The Methodology
of
Anthropological Comparisons

VIKING FUND PUBLICATIONS IN ANTHROPOLOGY

Number Fifty-three   Colin M. Turnbull, *Editor*

The
Methodology
of
Anthropological
Comparisons

AN ANALYSIS OF
COMPARATIVE METHODS
IN SOCIAL AND CULTURAL ANTHROPOLOGY

Gopāla Śaraṇa

Published for The Wenner-Gren Foundation for Anthropological Research Inc.

The University of Arizona Press   Tucson, Arizona

About the Author . . .

GOPĀLA ŚARAṆA, Professor and Chairman of the Department of Anthropology at Karnatak University, India, in 1974, has long had primary interest in methodological problems in anthropology. He has studied anthropology at Lucknow University under the late distinguished Professor D. N. Majumdar, received further training at Harvard University, and taught at Lucknow University, Panjab University, and the University of California, Santa Barbara. He is co-editor of *Indian Anthropology: Essays in The Memory of D. N. Majumdar* and the co-author of *Pragitihasa,* a Hindi book on prehistory. Believing that anthropologists should relate to philosophy of science, the author, in most of his other publications, deals with methodological and theoretical issues.

THE UNIVERSITY OF ARIZONA PRESS

JK

Contents

v

Preface

This volume is an attempt at a methodological analysis. Even now, books on the methodology of anthropology are rare, though in several of their titles, the words 'method' and 'methodology' may appear. S. F. Nadel's *The Foundations of Social Anthropology,* taken as a whole, is still a notable exception.

An interest in comparative methods was aroused in me two decades ago when I was a student of the late Professor D. N. Majumdar at the Lucknow University for the master's degree in anthropology. I was intrigued by the use of the term *"the* comparative method" by the nineteenth-century evolutionists, by Franz Boas and by A. R. Radcliffe-Brown. Their perspectives of and approaches to studying anthropology seemed to be so different. Milton Singer's report of the discussion on Schapera's paper in a Wenner-Gren Supper Conference convinced me further that it was not correct to talk of *the* comparative method. In spite of its antiquated title Ackerknecht's (1954) essay and Kroeber's comments on it acquainted me with some historical background of anthropological comparisons. From the very beginning I disagreed with Oscar Lewis's contention that there were no comparative methods in anthropology. According to him, these are only *comparisons* in cultural anthropology.

At Harvard University I was able to pursue my interests in comparative methods further and in a more systematic manner. Reading relevant literature on linguistics further strengthened my conviction that there were several comparative methods in social-cultural anthropology and in linguistics. I published an essay in the *Anthropological Quarterly* (Śaraṇa 1965) on the above theme. I must confess that not even one American linguist responded to my invitation to comment on and criticize my thesis. Most linguists — including linguistic anthropologists — still prefer to talk of *the* comparative method in linguistics. To them, my plea that there were several comparative methods in linguistics might have seemed unconventional or even bizarre.

I am deeply indebted to Professor Cora DuBois for encouragement and guidance. She taught me how to ask simple though meaningful questions. I am grateful to Professor Israel Scheffler of the Harvard School of Education for guiding my readings in philosophy of science. I thank Professor Michael Scriven, now of the University of California at Berkeley, for all the beneficial discussions I had with him on many methodological issues. I am also thankful to Professor A. Richard Diebold, Jr., for all the encouragement I received from him while I was at Harvard. I am really grateful to Dr. Colin M. Turnbull for compelling me to rethink and to take the argument to its logical conclusion. But I must state categorically that the present author alone should be held responsible for any flaws or shortcomings.

I dedicate this work to my father with all due reverence and ask for his blessings.

G. S.

CHAPTER 1

Terms of Reference

THE PURPOSE OF THE STUDY

Empirical social research and research procedures have received little or scant attention from philosophers of science, most of whom are preoccupied with the natural sciences. Not infrequently their recommendations for all the empirical sciences are based on the philosophers' acquaintance with the subject-matter, concepts, and procedures of the natural sciences. For instance, many textbooks on logic contain a few pages on the comparative method. These accounts are neither good 'reconstructed logic' nor do they refer to the 'logics-in-use' in the social sciences.

According to Abraham Kaplan, a *reconstructed logic* examines, evaluates, and looks for what is omitted or is not done. It is concerned not with what scientists actually do, but with what ideally they should do. "The reconstruction idealizes the logic of science only in showing us what it would be if it were extracted and refined to utmost purity" (Kaplan 1964:11). A *logic-in-use* is different from such a formulation by a philosopher or a philosophically minded scientist. Every scientist is aware of and practices the rules of inquiry generally acceptable to his fellow scientists. In their operations "scientists and philosophers use a logic — they have a cognitive style which is more or less logical" (Kaplan 1964:8). This is a *logic-in-use*.

The purpose of our inquiry is to make an analytical study of the different comparative methods. It will deal with the subject-matter, the purpose, and the techniques or procedures used by the anthropologist in his comparisons. It will, thus, be a study of logics-in-use of anthropological comparative studies.

1

The discussion of a scientific procedure would be incomplete without an examination of what lies behind it. In this connection I shall discuss concept and conceptualization as well as the traditional problem of inductive and deductive reasonings and their respective places in science. The notion of causation or antecedent-consequent approach also needs to be commented upon. These and other factors have a validity in the perspective of the stages through which a scientific discipline passes. It will be fruitful to indicate here what is meant when the terms hypothesis and theory are used.

There is a lack of clarity in the use of the terms technique, method, and methodology. They will be defined to facilitate our discussion of the comparative methods. The reasons for confusion about 'the comparative method' will be pointed out. It will be indicated that the comparative point of view and comparative sciences are different from comparative method. In this chapter, finally, we shall elaborate the implications of three basic questions about all comparative methods: what is compared, why, and how?

CONCEPT, CONCEPTION, AND CONCEPTUALIZATION

A concept is represented by a word (i.e., a term). A number of utterances are grouped together under such a term. A *concept* is meaningful in so far as the scientist attaches meaning to it within a certain context. A concept (term) may have several meanings; or, in Wittgenstein's metaphor, there may be a "family of meanings" (quoted in Kaplan 1964:48). A *concept* is a device used for arranging or collating empirical material. As Kaplan says, it "marks out the paths" of research. But by its very range it restricts the nature and the results of an inquiry.

A scientist has his own conception of a concept. It means that the same term or concept may convey different though related meanings to different scientists. A concept is a construct and is thus impersonal and timeless. A *conception* is one particular use of the family of meanings of a concept and it attributable to a particular person.

A third related term is conceptualization. Unlike a concept or a conception, conceptualization is a way or a process. It is through conceptualization that we attach meaning to any scientific term. According to the need of the occasion, *conceptualization* may consist of analysis, classification, or interrelation of a set of attributes or a combination of all of these. It is a procedure by which the comprehension of a problem is arrived at. It may be given a wider connotation to include understanding of a set of concepts, their interrelation and interpretation for solution of the problem at hand. When properly done, a conceptualization anticipates the result.

DEDUCTIVE AND INDUCTIVE REASONING

Deduction is often sharply contrasted with induction. It is not unusual to regard deduction a method of the a priori and to consider mathematics as an example. The natural and the social sciences, on the other hand, are said to be inductive or a posteriori sciences. But the present day logicians and scientists are aware that such a cut-and-dried division is not feasible.

In deductive reasoning certain broad and general statements (which may be either inductive conclusions or hypothetical concepts, laws, or regularities to suitable cases or classes of such cases) constitute the premises. Through defined logical steps the conclusions follow from the premises, i.e., the conclusions are implied in the premises. A deductive conclusion needs no further verification. Its 'certainty' is only of the procedure by which the conclusion is drawn. It does not imply the justification of the premises.

Inductive reasoning occupies an eminent place in "all adaptive behavior and in all inquiries into matters of fact" (Nagel 1961:xi). Induction is often defined as a procedure by which one arrives from particular to general or from less general to more general. It is the most important type of inductive inference but not the only one. One may proceed from particulars to a new particular (Von Wright 1957:1). Induction really means a reasoning from the known to the unknown. Carnap aptly puts it: "I mean here by inductive reasoning all forms of reasoning or inference where the conclusion goes beyond the content of the premises and therefore cannot be stated with certainty" (1953:189).

C. D. Broad once called inductive reasoning the 'glory of Science' and the 'scandal of Philosophy.' Russell calls it the most important postulate of science. Since Hume first voiced his objections many philosophers find it 'impossible' to justify induction. Russell is convinced that induction must have some kind of validity. But he holds that "the problem of showing how and why it is valid remains unsolved" (quoted in Von Wright 1957:177). Von Wright himself holds that Hume's skepticism does not pose a real problem. It has arisen because of the confusing language in which it is formulated. This philosophical debate is not without significance for science. It demonstrates clearly that inductive reasoning, though basic, is not the last word in scientific procedure.

Induction may be looked at as a procedure by which discoveries are made. It may also be reckoned as a relation between evidence and conclusion. The 'justification' of induction is not the same thing as that of deduction. Inductive conclusions cannot be as certain as the deductive ones: ". . . however formulated, it must yield the result that a correlation which has not been found false has at least a certain assignable probability of being always true" (Russell quoted in Von Wright 1957:177).

A few words about the meaning and place of probability in inductive reasoning is warranted here. Carnap considers probability the fundamental concept of inductive logic (1953:190). Statistical probability is different from inductive probability. Statistical probability is closely connected with frequency and can be empirically established by observations. It is "a certain quantitative physical characteristic of physical systems" (Carnap 1953:190).

An inductive probability is not merely a statement derived from observations or based on them. It expresses relations between a hypothesis and a body of evidence which is the result of actual or possible observations. It is expressed not in frequencies but in terms of the degree of confirmation of the hypothesis relative to the evidence. In Carnap's view, the statement of inductive probability expresses a logical relation and it does not require empirical testing. Thus it is like the logical relations in deductive logic. Carnap says that "inductive probability means in a sense partial deducibility" (1953:193). For example, when the value of inductive probability is close to 1 the hypothesis is nearly deducible from the evidence, though not quite so, because the relation is close to the relation of deducibility.

CAUSATION (ANTECEDENT-CONSEQUENT APPROACH)

In its very broad sense, 'causal connection' may mean any kind of lawfulness or orderliness in the course of events. The sciences dealing in change aim to discover causal connection in this sense. In a narrower sense, it means a law of invariable succession. It is a stronger connotation than a probabilistic correlation.

In J. S. Mills methodology of science the search for causal connection had a predominant place. He was following Francis Bacon when he held that one never acquired new knowledge by deductive reasoning. In Mill's opinion induction aims at discovering causes and effects. But it is not necessarily so. R. M. Eaton points out that cause and effect are not logical categories. They are rather "recalcitrant metaphysical ideas" which disappear from the more advanced sciences (1931:508). The inductive procedure is directed toward the proof of all generalizations rather than the special type called 'causal.' To restrict induction to the search of causal laws is out of step with the essence of Mill's own view on induction.

In common parlance, a cause is taken to be that which makes things happen. The nature of a thing or its characteristics belonging to it are relevant to the causal situation. The causal characteristic of a thing is its distinctive behavior in relation to other things. Things have causal relation but they do not change on their own. No two causal situations are exactly alike. A system whose parts are in mutual dependence has a causal dependence although in common parlance it is not recognized to be so.

A cause sometimes means a condition, manipulable by human beings. At other times it may be a condition near to or remote from the effect in space and time or an important and interesting condition (Black 1952:325). For the formulation of a causal law the following four conditions should be fulfilled. First, whenever the alleged cause occurs so does the alleged effect. This principle of invariability is based upon the belief that 'nature is uniform.' Second, the relation holds between spatially contiguous events. Third, the temporal character implies that the causal event is antecedent to the effect and is also continuous with it. Fourth, the relation between the cause and the effect is asymmetrical.

Russell disagrees with the view that whenever distinction between cause and effect is applicable to a causal situation the cause precedes the effect. In his opinion an effect may be before, simultaneous with, or after a cause because there is no scientific importance to its being after the cause. He and Stebbing both hold that the notion of causation is not of critical importance in advanced sciences like gravitational astronomy. In such a discipline it is replaced by the notion of 'functional dependence.' This fact is usually overlooked by some social scientists who believe that causation is the essence of scientific procedure.

Michael Scriven thinks causal relations hold only between particular events and occurrences without the necessity of a covering law to account for them. Black sums up the prevailing view that something's being a cause involves an underlying generalization (1952:324). In other words, in a scientific sense Q is said to be caused by P in that there is a law L and when from the conjunction of L and an account of P it may be possible to deduce Q (Pap 1962:271).

In order that a causal correlation be well-defined it must have both sufficient and necessary causes or conditions. This makes predictions applicable both retrospectively and prospectively. For example, N is a necessary condition of N′, if, when N is false N′ is also false, i.e., a necessary condition of N is one without which it cannot be true. When one says that C, to take another example, is the necessary and sufficient condition of the occurrence of E one means that the occurrence of C is essential to the occurrence of E. This last formulation is unacceptable to Peter Alexander. He believes that the notion of cause is concerned with temporal order while that of necessary and sufficient conditions is not (1963:99).

STAGES THROUGH WHICH AN EMPIRICAL DISCIPLINE PASSES

Physics, astronomy, and mathematics made their debut as scientific disciplines about two thousand years ago. Chemistry and geology could attain this status only in the last two hundred years. The science of living is old. But a real breakthrough, leading it in the direction of its phenomenal progress, came only in the last century and a half.

A close look at the different sciences reveals some sort of regularity in patterns of their development and the degree of their sophistication. The treatment of the strategic levels of the subject-matter and the type of conclusions arrived at clearly demonstrate the above facts. Kroeber (1954:273-74) has worked out the following stages in the development of science:

(1) Description of properties of form and substance of the phenomenon (phenomenological stage);
(2) Ordering or classification based upon analysis of their structures (classificatory stage);
(3) Tracing of their changes or events; and
(4) Formulation of process ('historical'-processual stage for both [3] and [4]).

Biology before Darwin had only reached the first two stages. In other words, it was on the phenomenological-classificatory level. Linnaeus performed the great task of bringing order by his classifications. But his species concept was static. Cuvier furthered the work of comparison by conscious search of 'types' or patterns. A change from static classification to dynamic change and process came through the theory of organic evolution. It has attained greater sophistication in the present century due to the contribution made by genetics.

The nineteenth-century anthropologists aped biology in their attempts to classify cultural materials. For an important reason their efforts were not too successful. In their disciplines there were no reliable empirical studies of form (or structure) and substance on which their classifications could be based. Due to this failure social-cultural anthropology today is without comprehensive and generally acceptable scheme(s) of classification. The emphasis on fieldwork for every professional anthropologist, in this century, has resulted in a good number of descriptive-analytical studies of form and function in human societies and cultures. The subject-matter of social-cultural anthropology is expanding. New types of societies and cultures are being examined. These may eventually lead to some sort of viable classification, though at present, unlike other scientists, anthropologists are tracing changes without classificatory devices. Kroeber has aptly remarked that a full-fledged 'historical' science of anthropology is still ahead of us. Attempts to formulate generalized process, including that by Kroeber himself, have not been to successful up to date.

According to Northrop there are two stages of a science in terms of the procedures of research and the language of theoretical formula tions. In the first, or the natural history stages of a science, there is a great emphasis on fieldwork. The language of presentation remains less critical and the descriptions contain the largest number of empirical facts. In Northrop's second, or deductively formulated, stage a theoretical sophistication is visible in more critical language. There is scarch for minimal theoretical antecedents and 'primitive' concepts from which all other concepts of the subject-matter can be derived by definition. With the operational definitions, stress is laid on indirect ways of verification rather than direct empiricism (Northrop 1964:195 & 196).

HYPOTHESIS AND THEORY

Both laymen and scientists conduct inquiries. The former deal with the commonsense level of inquiry. The scientist, on the other hand, concerns himself with technical problems. Their comprehension and resolution require greater background knowledge and complex notions. In both kinds of inquiry there may be an underlying supposition which binds together, conceptually, a set of facts which are to be accounted for. Such a supposition, formulated as a proposition, yields certain suggestions. It may be expected to occur under some determinate conditions. A proposition like this is neither true nor false. But the suggestions emanating from it can be tested and evidence may be provided to accept or reject the original supposition. Wolf calls it a 'working idea' (1962:159).

Facts are properly accounted for if they are organized into a system. A layman's interests are practical. He is satisfied by linking habitually one experience with another. But a scientist is willing to undertake an industrious analysis of the whole situation in which he is interested. He needs well-formulated hypotheses generated by one or more working ideas.

A *hypothesis,* presented as a proposition in which a connection or a relationship is foreseen between certain phenomena, is stated in such a way that it can either be confirmed or confuted by independent evidence.

It may be argued by some that since science is based on experience, a scientific hypothesis ought to originate only in some concrete experience of objects or events. Apart from concrete experience, a hypothesis may arise in a dream, in imagination, in an intuition, or by trial and error. Irrespective of the way in which a hypothesis originated, in order to be effective it should be capable of deductive development (Alexander 1963:107). Deduction plays an important role in the elimination of unsuitable hypotheses and in the confirmation of the remaining.

Our statements about a hypothesis are not very different from what is generally accepted in the 'hypothetico-deductive method' of science. According to this method a scientist arrives at a set of postulates covering the phenomena he is interested in: "a combination of careful observable consequences are deduced which are tested by observation and experiment." Kaplan (1964) has pointed out that the value of the reconstructions of hypothetico-deductive logic lies, not in their mathematical precision or elegance, but, in their capacity to illuminate the *logic-in-use.*

Karl Popper (1959) has worked out his own variant of the hypothetico-deductive method. According to him a hypothesis is empirically testable only if some observational statements can be formulated which contradict the hypothesis. Popper considers falsification very basic to his method. To him a hypothesis is not verified when it is confirmed, but when some of its rival hypotheses are falsified. Hempel, Barker, and others have pointed out that this is not a very satisfactory way to entertain hypotheses in science. Any empirical social researcher who champions Popper's thesis pays little or no attention to the latter's criticism of inductivism. Popper holds that there are many difficulties encountered by induction which cannot meet the requirements of logical correctness. So Popper is for eliminating induction from the so-called inductive sciences and for replacing it by the deductive method. Kotarbinska (1962) has shown why Popper's endeavors have failed.

Logicians and philosophers of science consider a scientific theory to be a deductive system. It is an ideal which is not easy to attain. It is, as Nagel says, "a task which, though often difficult to practice, is realizable in principle" (1961:91). In this limiting case of a rigorously formulated deductive theory, the fundamental assumptions are set forth as a constellation of uninterpreted or abstract postulates. They define the basic terms (i.e., theoretical terms) of the theory.

The deductive superstructure of a theory is expressed through a calculus or a formal axiomatic system. The empirically verifiable generalizations are at the bottom and should be derivable from the initial abstract postulates placed at the top. Every principle of deduction corresponds to 'a rule of symbolic manifestation' based on a sequence of sentences (or formulae) containing axioms (or initial postulates) and theorems (or sentences deduced from the axioms). For explanation and prediction the theoretical notions ought to be related with observables. But a substantial body of deductive theory consists of the postulates or derivations from them which are not based on direct observation. The observational-empirical restraints may be applicable only to the lower levels of the theoretical superstructure. Instead of being a drawback this may provide more maneuverability. In case of conflict between observations and the theory, some reworking even at the top may be necessary.

In a recent article Braithwaite suggests that any scientific deductive system should be called a theory. When the theory is small, he argues in the same context, or applies to an 'isolated' field, it may be called a *theorita* or a diminutive theory (Braithwaite 1962:224). But he is also aware that in the social sciences even semi-formalized (i.e., expressed by a partial calculus) theory is rare. An illustration of this comes from Radcliffe-Brown. In his view a theory has three aspects: (1) There is a set of analytical concepts; (2) they are defined in relation to the concrete reality of a certain class; (3) there is a logical relation between the concepts. It may be noted that he does not speak of deduction; instead he introduces the idea of a system of classification and a set of rules of procedure (Radcliffe-Brown 1958:166).

A *theory* in the social sciences is not a very rigorously formulated deductive system. It is usually called a 'scheme of interpretation' or even a 'frame of reference.' In this broad sense a theory is a means to unify the established regularities and to prune them, to enable wider generalizations so that even unanticipated data may be covered. In a way a theory is conjectural in contrast to the empirical facts because it is a symbolic reconstruction. It is not suggested here that a theory has nothing to do with experience; it is, in fact, rooted in experience. We agree with Kaplan that a theory involves a conceptual "constructing from the selected materials something with no counterpart in experience at all" (1964:297).

From the point of view of content a molecular or microtheory may be distinguished from a molar or macrotheory. A macroeconomic theory, for instance, deals with an industry or a complete economic system. A microtheory in economics may be concerned with the roles of individuals in the functioning of an economy. Another basis on which to separate lower level from higher level theories is the degree of abstractness. In conjunction with this are the extent and length of deductions derivable from the theory. In the social sciences a theory is not always viewed in hypothetico-deductive terms. So not without justification in many cases, a microtheory — both in depth and range — is preferred.

TECHNIQUE, METHOD, AND METHODOLOGY

Logician A. Wolf says that any mode of investigation by which the sciences have been developed deserves to be called a scientific method. But he distinguishes the *technical* methods from the *logical* methods (Wolf 1962:28). The former are the methods of manipulating and measuring the phenomena under investigation and the conditions suitable for their fruitful observation (Wolf 1962:28). By the logical methods he means the methods of reasoning according to the nature of the data (Wolf 1962:29). He considers the technical methods mainly auxiliary to the logical methods of science.

Today Wolf's distinctions are further elaborated by the use of three related, though distinct, terms — technique, methods, and methodology. A *technique* is a device, a means or a procedure — verbal or mechanical — for collecting and processing data in the particular contexts of a scientific inquiry. A scientific technique may be used for more than one purpose. The techniques of a science are the means by which the professionally acceptable work of that science is carried out. Some techniques commonly used in social science research are interviews, case studies, observation, statistics, etc.

A *method* is more than an interrelation of a number of techniques, or a technique general enough to be used in several disciplines.

Herskovits insightfully asserts that the term method indicates more than the procedures utilized to execute a given research project (1954:5). By definition a method implies a goal or an end to be achieved. It is a system, a complete set of the rules of procedure, employed in realizing the given goal. By appropriate choice, the suitable research techniques become a part of any such set of rules.

A *methodology* is the analytical study of methods. Specific studies are examined here as to the procedures adopted, the assumptions made, and the results obtained. The nature of the generalizations, if any, and the explanations, if attempted, are also scrutinized.

The methodological premise for inductive research was codified by J. S. Mill in his *Logic*. He called them "the four methods of inductive inquiry." The first three — the Methods of Agreement, of Difference, and of Residues — are methods of (qualitative) elimination. For a successful application of these methods it is essential to have controls and to produce circumstances artificially. These methods, therefore, become unsuitable for those social science disciplines in which, as in anthropology, the social phenomena are treated in real life situations without any alteration. In Mill's Method of Concomitant Variations, quantitative co-variation of circumstances, not elimination, is required (1911: 263). In his *Rules* Durkheim (1938) raised the latter to the level of the only research method available for sociological studies. He argued in favor of qualitative co-variation to demonstrate the extent to which similarities or differences in any one feature were accompanied by others. In formal terms such empirically established relations can be represented by this formula: where P, and Q, for in situations a^1, a^2, a^3 . . . . . there are P and Q and in situations a^4, a^5, a^6 . . . . . there are P-changed and Q-changed.

Mill's four methods of 'experimental inquiry' are comparative methods in the sense that, in some form, comparison is used in all of them. Are these 'methods' the only methods of discovery as well as of proof or confirmation? Whewell, a contemporary of Mill's, was of the opinion that the latter's 'methods' were not good for either. They took for granted the most difficult thing, the reduction of data into the formulae referred to by Mill in his 'methods.' Mill defended his formulations vigorously. It seems that the relations between things can be discovered, as hypotheses can be formulated, with or without a comparative method. But a comparative method is necessarily involved in establishing a proof. In other words, comparative methods are the sole methods of proof, although not the only means of discovery. In any methodological study these considerations must be reckoned with.

COMPARISON

We cannot say we are comparing if we simply set things side by side without deriving any results from it. To compare means to examine two or more things to bring out the resemblance and/or differences in their characteristic qualities.

Comparison is a basic aspect of human thought. In the sciences it plays a vital role. In all analogy, classification, definition, and division, comparison is involved in one form or the other. J. S. Mill's four methods of inductive inquiry are also based on comparison. But comparison *as such* means only dealing with the material to extract some knowledge. Much more than this is meant when a term like 'comparative point of view,' 'comparative science' or 'comparative method' is used.

Comparative Point of View

During the sixteenth and seventeenth centuries the European travelers and explorers brought home information about non-European peoples. The comparative point of view in the philosophical and humanistic disciplines of that time resulted from reflections upon the numerous ways in which man could satisfy his wants and tackle his problems. The illuminating works of the Enlightenment such as Voltaire's *Essai sur les moeurs* and Montesquieu's *De l'esprit des lois* resulted from the comparative point of view. They indicated a lessening rigidity about the sacredness of the mores and values of the Western world as well as an increased secular spirit. This comparative point of view should not be confused with 'the comparative method.'

Comparative Sciences

The all-embracing field of social philosophy broke up, between 1700 and 1825, into such disciplines as economics, politics, jurisprudence, etc. The idea of comparative sciences became prominent as objectivity increased and more stress was laid on secular progress. It was a significant event because many subjects like jurisprudence, politics, mythology, etc., had until then been concerned only with the Western institutions. This broadened interest was indicated by the label 'comparative.' Anatomy and physiology too had become comparative. What was implied by comparative anatomy was the comparison of different kinds of organisms, in order to trace the biological relationships between them. The method appropriate for this task was called *the comparative method.*

The notion of the comparative sciences included more than merely a comparative point of view. It was held that the similarities established through comparison could be accounted for by tracing descent from a common source. In other words, the early comparative sciences had a genetic or developmental 'theory.' An anticipation of this line of thought can be seen in Sir W. Jones' projections of genetic relationship between Sanskrit, Greek, and Latin in the eighteenth century. But the substantive work in comparative anatomy gave more impetus to applying 'the method' (of genetic relations) in other fields. Comparative anatomy was the 'glamor science' and 'the comparative method' became the ruler of science in the nineteenth century (Ackerknecht 1954:118).

COMPARATIVE METHOD AND ANTHROPOLOGY

The theory of organic evolution was the great achievement of the comparative method in the biological sciences, particularly comparative anatomy and taxonomy. 'The comparative method' was declared as the greatest discovery of the nineteenth century by Max Muller and E. A. Freeman. The method yielded valuable results in the fields where things were derived from a common source or where the institutions of a people of common origin were investigated, e.g., evolutionary biology, comparative jurisprudence, comparative philology, comparative mythology, etc. Anthropology could not remain unaffected by this intellectual movement.

After physical and social-cultural anthropology became separated, they both turned evolutionist. 'The comparative method' and 'classical' (evolutionist) anthropology, were so closely linked that the two were considered equivalents. As we saw above, in 'the comparative method' the idea of accounting for the similarities by descent from a common source was considered crucial. Several extensions of this idea can be seen in the realm of nineteenth-century social-cultural anthropology, e.g., search for first origins, survivals, fixed developmental stages, etc. But, in fact, no definite common origin for the primitive peoples could be established. So in social-cultural anthropology 'the comparative method' was used to formulate historical inferences even though historical evidence was lacking.

An interest in similarities should be distinguished from that in differences. The classical anthropologists were not really interested in accounting for similarities. The psychic unity of mankind was a necessary assumption in order to make comparisons since one cannot scientifically compare non-comparables. Their interest was to account for differences within a larger 'theory' of socio-cultural evolution, based in turn upon analogic reasoning from organic evolution. The psychic unity of mankind, though a partially valid assumption, remained unexamined in the hands of the unilinear evolutionists.

When evolutionist doctrines in social-cultural anthropology were attacked by protagonists of diffusion, 'the comparative method' also fell in disrepute. The diffusionists were objecting to the nomenclature. They used comparison extensively themselves. But they would not give it that name. 'The comparative method' had become the method to trace 'origins' on the basis of evolutionary principles. They repudiated the facile analogy to biologic evolution as it was popularly held in the nineteenth century, i.e., of a unilinear development from the simple to the complex. In some ways the diffusionists went further in developing comparative approaches than the 'classical' evolutionists. Their approach is sometimes known as the culture historical 'method' of ethnology.[1] There may be some objection to the use of the word 'method' here. It may be argued that the culture history approach was not a 'method' and 'the comparative method' was still in use. The diffusionists repudiated cross analyzing from biology because their 'theory' changed. They compared, but the technical details, the types of materials, and the purpose of grouping them was conceived in the framework of diffusion. As a later section of this chapter makes clear, it is not possible to say that 'the comparative method' was still in use, even though comparisons were made by the diffusionists. Their comparative method was entirely different.

In 1896 Boas pointed out 'the limitations of the comparative method.' He recommended a modified use of comparison within a small well-defined geographical area. He called his method a 'historical method.' It "duly recognizes the results obtained by comparative studies." Likewise, Murdock uses statistical techniques to give a new dimension to his comparisons. But he prefers to call them a cross-cultural survey. Radcliffe-Brown, on the other hand, calls his method "the comparative method in social anthropology." He holds that comparisons can be made for two quite different purposes and that correspondingly there are two separate methods (1951:15) thus admitting the existence of two comparative methods. But expressly he talks only of his own version, as if it were the sole comparative method in social-cultural anthropology.

---

1. This is the title which W. Schmidt chose for his book. It was translated into English in 1939. Since F. Graebner's *Methode der Ethnologie* is not translated, Schmidt's book remains the only methodological statement about the Vienna School available to the speakers of English.

There are thus some anthropologists who use a type of comparison but they do not want to call it a comparative method. There are others who call their approach 'the comparative method.' The latter seems to imply that no other comparative method exists in anthropology except the one advocated. Another group of anthropologists realizes that the differences in various uses of comparison should be accepted. It is obvious that all these cannot be grouped under the rubric, 'the comparative method.' Oscar Lewis, on the other hand, holds that there are only comparisons in anthropology, no comparative methods. He insists that the distinction proposed by him is not merely semantic. In his view it highlights the fact that "the method of comparison is only one aspect of a comparison" (Lewis 1955:259). We agree with him that the difference is not only semantic because Lewis confuses technique with method. He is not alone in doing so.

Anthropology is called a comparative discipline. One of the two justifications of this is the following: By convention and established tradition of doing fieldwork in a culture other than one's own, the anthropologist uses a comparative framework in his study. In other words, there is much implicit comparison both in data-gathering and data-processing. Our concern in the present study is not to reflect upon such implicit comparisons even though methodologically they are quite significant.

The second justification of anthropology's being a comparative discipline is for work in the library rather than in the field. From the days of unilinear evolution anthropologists have utilized the available ethnographic materials to serve many different ends. There are marked differences in the ways these ends have been attained. The common feature of all these ventures is the fact that, with very few exceptions, they all involve intercultural or cross-cultural explicit comparison. It will be too much to expect that all these comparisons would follow the hypothetico-deductive procedure. Hypothesis-testing is only one of the several purposes for which comparison is made.

THE THREE BASIC QUESTIONS

The first question is *what* should one compare. To a great extent it depends upon the interests of the researcher. Traits and institutions have one thing in common. Both are treated as unit categories, although they are further divisible. The problem here is isolation and definition of a trait. We shall see how a trait is compared in its different forms, such as, a biologic given category (reproduction), a material manifestation (pottery or basketry), a set of rules (games like Patolli and Pachisi), or a relationship (mother's brother). Comparison of institutions is quite common. 'Social organization' as a topic of comparison has its own specificity. A second class of units of comparison may be aggregates. One group of aggregates can be defined and located empirically. Communities, 'culture areas,' and cultural wholes are some examples of empiric aggregates. Cultural wholes pose unique problems of definition and representation. Another group of aggregates is conceptual. Totemism and 'culture complex' (particularly *Kulturkreise*) are good examples. It is possible that the researcher may treat these as if they were empirically definable.

The second question is *why* should one compare. In other words, what is the aim of a comparison? It may in some cases be *inferential history*. In one of its phases the distribution of traits in a limited region may be traced as in Spier's Sun Dance and Klimek's culture element distribution studies. Some sort of 'universal history' like that attempted by the classical evolutionists is another variety on a grander scale. *Typology* or *classification* is another purpose for which comparisons are undertaken. A typology may be descriptive-analytical like those of Lowie, Murdock, or Radcliffe-Brown. It may also aim at developmental stages, e.g., Redfield's transformations of the primitive world and the growth of cities. *Generalization* is yet another purpose of comparison, e.g., one may want to test a hypothesis, or to formulate a generalization of limited applicability in the range as well as in the subject-matter. Universal laws, more general in nature, are also the goals which some anthropologists, such as Radcliffe-Brown, would like to attain. *Generalized process* can be formulated in, at least, two ways: in one, two synchronic comparative studies of the some society, undertaken at two different times by the same or different researchers, may be used to formulate processes of change. A concern with the diachronic regularity over long periods of time may give us the process of growth or development. Kroeber and Steward, for instance, are particularly interested in it.[2]

The third question is *how* does one make comparisons.[3] This is the least clear of all the three aspects of comparison we have mentioned.

---

2. We are aware that the goals for which comparisons are made are inadequately stated. Some of the terms used are not current and need to be defined. We shall take up this task of clarification and elaboration in one of the chapters to follow.

3. By the 'how' of comparison we mean the procedure adopted. It need not be confused with the goals of comparison. Two different procedures may be used to achieve the same goal.

One way is to compare by means of *illustration*. Following this procedure a set of already earmarked categories or a preconceived scheme of interpretation is supported with illustrations selected according to the 'convenience' of the researcher. Another procedure is to compare within a *universe of limited discourse*. The distinctive feature of this approach is to cover the total universe without any sampling. The studies of this type may compare divisions of the same culture, may cover units in a region, or may deal with a whole continent. A third comparative method adopts an *explicitly statistical procedure*. Based on sampling, the contemporary version of this approach professes to take into account all the primitive societies on a worldwide scale.

Units of Comparison

Our concern here is with what is compared. There is great diversity in the subject-matter and topics of comparison. This should not come as a surprise if one keeps in view the expanse of anthropology. Moreover, much depends, with regard to what is compared, upon the interest of the researcher. Hobhouse, Wheeler, and Ginsberg (1915) faced this problem squarely. They selected a 'tribe' as a unit of their comparisons. But they faced difficulties in defining a tribe.

The scale of the societies/cultures becomes a factor which needs to be reckoned with. Following the Wilsons (1945) and Mair (1963) the scale is determined, we think, by the range of socio-political and economic activities of the people. They depend upon the type of technology and the means of travel, transport, and communication. In a small-scale society, the same persons and groups take part in the most important purposes of life (Mair 1963:13). Most anthropological comparisons do not mix up scales. The fact to be noted, then, is the unit of comparison. A unit may be a trait, an institution, or a community or an aggregate of these. It may be further divisible into part-units or items.

COMPARISON OF TRAITS AND INSTITUTIONS

The Problem of What Is a Trait

A culture-trait is a meaningfully identifiable unit of a culture isolated by observation in time and space. A trait is a construct. Its form is determined by the context, not by any quality inherent in it. Though it is taken as the minimal significant unit of a culture, it cannot be delimited absolutely. Any trait is thus somewhat arbitrarily devised. A trait may be further divided in smaller parts. But they cannot themselves be considered traits as they do not remain the significant minimal components of a culture. A trait may be a material or a nonmaterial aspect of a culture or even a biologic given.

Trait as a Biologic Given Category

Sex is a fact characteristic of all mankind. Menstruation, conception, pregnancy, childbirth, and lactation are physiological events which know no national, racial, or cultural boundaries. One study of sexual behavior (i.e., "behavior involving stimulation and excitation of the sexual organs," Ford and Beach 1951:4) deals with the physiological factors involved as well as the biological factors underlying various kinds of sexual activities. The data were obtained from 190 different societies and from mammals representing "many different species from rats and mice to man's nearest living relatives, the great apes" (Ford and Beach 1951:1). In this study one finds a mixing up of societies at different scales with nonhuman groups. The nature of this study resulted in subordination of the socio-cultural aspects to the physiological ones.

Using the ethnographic materials contained in the files of the Cross-Cultural Survey, another study takes up the task of analyzing beliefs and practices about reproduction in sixty-four human societies around the globe (Ford 1945). The focus of attention is the customs which surround the reproductive cycle in the primitive societies. The data on such items as menstruation, coitus, conception, pregnancy, childbirth, and early parenthood are compared to see if there are any "functional relationships between customs and the physical processes of reproduction" (Ford 1945:86).

Trait as a Material Manifestation

The study of material culture is not very fashionable in anthropology these days. It may partly be due to what Kroeber calls a recent social science influence on social-cultural anthropology. There is a singular lack of comparative studies of material traits. There are many well-known studies of the material culture of American Indian tribes but there is hardly any comparison therein. Lowie's *An Introduction to Cultural Anthropology* (1940) contains several chapters on material

aspects of culture, while Boas (1936) deals with a number of technological innovations and their development in his *General Anthropology*.
Otis T. Mason's (1931: 249-66) study of the 'types of basket weaves'
is an excellent example of a generalized account. His purpose there
is not to compare basket weaves of different cultures; it is to describe
handwoven and sewed types of basketry. The former is divisible into
checkerwork, twilled-work, wichwork, wrappedwork, and twinedwork.
This study is based on a comparison of specimens in the museum.
But what the reader is presented with is an account of the finished
typology. The names of the places where a certain type is found are
mentioned insignificantly. For example, twinework type is found in
British Columbia, Washington, Southern United States, and Central
America, as well as in Peru, Guiana, and Ecuador, etc. Basketry is
treated as an independent entity not as a trait of a culture.

A study dealing with a trait as a material manifestation within the
context of a culture has been done by C. S. Ford (1937). It is called
"A Sample Comparative Study of Material Culture." The receptacles
in two primitive cultures are compared. Techniques of production and
extent of their use are noted. Few differences in the use of the receptacles are found in the two cultures except one. The occurrence of
pottery is of far-reaching importance in one of the cultures. So pottery
is made the unit of a second set of comparison. The specific uses of
pottery in one culture are compared with the solutions to the same
problem in the other. It is also noted whether the solutions of the
second culture are used in the first culture. This comparison reveals the
place of pottery in the two cultures in particular and the solutions of
problems of retaining things in general.

Trait as a Set of Rules

A game is an easily identifiable culture trait. Unlike a material
trait a game is a set of rules. The apparent similarity between the
Aztec game called Patolli and the Hindu game of Pachisi was noted by
E. B. Tylor in 1878. His analysis of this 'similarity' is an early example
of comparison of a culture trait as a set of rules.

Tylor's first essay on this topic was entitled "On the Game of
Patolli in Ancient Mexico and its probable Asiatic Origin" (1878).
In general, cross-like tracks drawn on 'boards' or 'mats,' counters
determined by throwing of lots, and irregular scoring were found to be
similar between Patolli and Pachisi. In an article published later,
i.e. in 1896, he provided more weight to the relationship between the
two games of probability. His argument proceeds as follows: the

phenomena may be treated as independent if any comparison of their constituent units shows very little or no connection between them. The more numerous the similarities in the elements, the more likely it is that their combinations will not occur independently. In other words, the 'adhesions' between the elements should be necessary, not arbitrary or accidental. The relation of the Patolli-Pachisi group of games must be accounted for by diffusion before the Spanish conquest. It is improbable (to the sixth order of invention) that the following similar features between the two could have been invented independently: divining by lot and its application to sportive wager, the combination of several lots with the law of chances, the transfer of result to a counting board and the particular rules of moving and taking.

Tylor works out a general pattern based on the similarities of these elements. The isolability of the games or their integration with the respective cultures seems to pose no problem in this case. Tylor uses the similarities as noted proof of the genetic relation between Patolli and Pachisi. A careful study of the American Indian games led Steward Culin to the conclusion that they were the direct outgrowth of aboriginal institutions in America.

Kroeber, in 1931, supported Tylor's conclusion: "Their structural similarities in two-sided lot-throwing, count values dependent on frequency of lot combinations, a cruciform scoring circuit, the killing of opponents that are overtaken, etc., make out a strong case for a true homology and therefore a genetic unity of the two game forms, in spite of their geographical separation" (1931:149-51). In 1948 he considers the question still open. He argues that the structural similarities between Patolli and Pachisi are not discernible in other culture-traits which might have come to Mexico from Asia along with Pachisi. Tylor chose two traits in two far-flung regions and by postulating growth of one trait (Patolli) from the other (Pachisi) hoped to work out the inferential history of the former.

Trait as a Relationship

Junod held that the special relationship of mother's brother and sister's son among the patrilocal Ba Thonga indicated that some time in the past they were matrilocal. Opposed to this 'survival' hypothesis Radcliffe-Brown was of the opinion that what really mattered were the present relationships. His thesis was that a relationship could not be studied in isolation. So he saw a correlation between customs relating to the mother's brother and those relating to the father's sister and brother's son. From its title Radcliffe-Brown's "The Mother's Brother in South Africa" (1924) may appear to be a regional study. But the three main tribes mentioned for illustrative comparison are the Ba Thonga of Portuguese East Africa, the Nama Hottentots of South Africa, and the Tongans of Polynesia. Broadening the base of his comparison he says the relations with the mother's brother and the sister's son are of equal importance and can be accounted for in terms of certain fundamental principles, e.g., the equivalence of brothers or the unity of the sibling group. The tender feelings toward the mother are extended to the mother's brother and the sentiment of respect toward the father is extended to the father's sister. This conclusion seems to be a deduction from the principle he assumed at the beginning of the inquiry.

Comparison of Institutions

Institution refers to organized social behavior which is intentional, task-oriented (i.e., purposive), and standardized. In Nadel's opinion an institution is valid for a group and is activated by the latter (1951:118). It will be more appropriate to say that every institution has a personnel which may be a part of the group or the whole of it. Institutions are of many kinds, e.g., economic, educational, kinship, legal, magico-religious, political, recreational, scientific, etc.

The family is very commonly used for comparison. In one such comparative study the problem may be to ascertain the existence of the elementary family in a group of nonliterate cultures. The items of comparison here may be the modes of obtaining wives, the actual relations between parents and children, the sexual aspect of marriage, the mode of living, the kinship, the actual relation between husband and wife, and the economic unity of the 'family.' The study will show how intimate is the link of the elementary family with "a whole series of customs, beliefs and fundamental phenomena" (Malinowski 1963:293) in the cultures under investigation.

When the fact of existence of the elementary family is not in doubt and the quantitative data are available, a comparative study of the family may take into account such facts: the population structure, the system of mating relations, the composition of domestic groups, the distribution of children, the variety of domestic forms, etc. (Smith 1962). In a regional context a typological grouping of the family structures may be compared for these items, among others: the economic determinants, the ideology and principles of descent and succession, the marriage contract, the domestic authority, and the residential units (cp. Richards 1950).

Let us take two societies which have similar features as identical environment, related languages, identical kinship systems, similar political and economic organizations, belief in witchcraft, and the conception that it is unequivocally evil. The comparison is directed to find out whether the witches and their victims are only males or females or both. The differences, if any, between child-rearing practices and consequent infantile experiences may be examined as they may determine important cultural differences. It is interesting to compare two societies which share many common features but only one has witchcraft. The one society which has no witchcraft beliefs has a full and explicit mythology, not unlike the other society where the people are obsessed with the fear of witchcraft. In such a situation, it is obvious that the difference between the two societies can be understood better through a comparative study of some other item(s) like premarital sex relations (cp. Nadel 1952).

Comparison of 'Social Organization'

In our discipline social organization is variously defined. When it is not being contrasted with social structure, as proposed by Firth, it is supposed to refer to more than one institution. There are several cases of comparative study of social organization. We shall examine here a few to see what is included under this category.

One study may aim to bring up-to-date, for the layman, a summary of what was known in the twenties about primitive social organization (Lowie 1920:V). The extensive comparison made here is of parts of tribes, institutions, or groups. One purpose may be to establish some categories which are general enough for comparisons of all primitive tribes, e.g., marriage, polygamy, the family, kinship usages, the sib (or clan), the position of women, property, rank, government, justice, etc. Not all these categories were current before such a comparative study.

Another comparative study of social organization may first describe the 'general type.' Then the main varieties, serving as 'norms,' may be described. Other 'systems' in the same geographical area may be compared with the 'norms' next in terms of social structure. The categories used are: the family, horde, tribe, moiety, marriage classes, sections, pair, cycle, etc., or other suitable categories (Radcliffe-Brown 1930-31). The following framework was used to describe the 'norms.' It means that the emphasis was on kinship: the numbers and the names of the tribes included, the estimate of population, the sections, subsections and hordes, the kinship system including marriage and the totemic system without excluding the clan. When a more specific representation of social organization by kinship is stipulated, it may be covered under such headings as kinship terminology, kinship extensions, the household, the clan, and ceremonial organization (cp. Eggan 1950).

COMPARISON OF EMPIRIC AGGREGATES

By an empiric aggregate we mean a collection of categories or traits whose combination into a unity is not subject to the imagination of the researcher but can be referred to empirically. In this class we shall deal with communities, 'culture areas' and cultural wholes like civilizations.

Communities as Empiric Aggregates

Explicit comparison within the same culture is not common in anthropology. Even when the aspects dealt with are not of the same order, the common tendency is to present a rounded picture of the 'common' features. A comparison of communities is usually an intra-cultural study. If someone wants to find out the 'norm,' say, in the domestic organization of a tribe, one may choose two communities, or villages or townships for explicit comparison. Many common features between the two may be found. The two units chosen for comparison are at the same scale, i.e., they are at the same level of organization. If counting is possible the statistical data may be used. The units (communities) are compared on such items as the dwelling group, the generation depth, the household head, headship and social maturation, the forms of domestic unit, and place of kinship in it (cp. Fortes 1949).

A comparison of communities at different levels of organization, though belonging to the same overall culture, poses problems of an altogether different nature. The focus of attention in this case is dissimilar communities. So the items of comparison may be recon-structed types — either polar or on the same continuous scale. Such broad categories as medicine and magic, family organization, etc., may be used in conjunction with general concepts, e.g., folk and urban, individualization and secularization, organization and disorganization, for comparison. Redfield's (1941) study is an interesting example of such a comparison. In the heat of debating the concept of folk-urban continuum, the significance of such a comparison did not receive enough attention.

'Cultural Areas' as Empiric Aggregates

Clark Wissler's 'culture area' concept is descriptive and is not concerned with time depth. It envisages a static description of culture elements as they occur aggregated in space. Comparison is not essential to define the main characteristic traits of each culture area. But when Wissler talks about 'culture centers' the focus of attention changes. In the latter concept the areal culture aggregates are seen in relation with classifications of other culture centers and the distributions of individual culture traits. When specific culture traits are traced in the cultural setting of the past or the present, comparison is constantly involved. Wissler's (1926) use of the 'age and area' (or age-area) concept is to show how to infer time sequences from space distributions of isolable clusters of culture traits. This 'age-area' tool, used by Wissler and others, is not Wissler's 'invention.' It was known in biology long before Wissler applied it to anthropological data. But he deserves all credit, for it was empirically arrived at. A supplement to the documentary evidence of history and archaeological stratification, the 'age-area' concept serves as a useful device to infer time depth beyond the range of historical or archaeological evidence.

An interesting example of combination of the idea of a culture-complex with that of a culture area can be found in Leslie Spier's (1921) comparative study of the Sun Dance. Though individual traits form the basis of the study, their integration within the 'complex' is specifically noted. Nineteen Plains Indian tribes are included in the culture area. Like other studies by the American distributionists, a list of the elements which constitute the 'total' Sun Dance is prepared. Then the traits which constitute the Sun Dance of the individual Plains tribes are compared with this 'basic' list to find out the presence and absence of the elements of the Dance. In other words, the comparison is directed toward finding out the similarities and differences between the elements of the Dance and their differential manifestations in the different tribes of the culture area. When each Dance is compared with the total tribal system to which it belongs, it means that the problem of its cultural identity and integration is not completely forgotten. In Spier's study both material and nonmaterial items were included. His main interest was in working out the psychological and historical factors which impeded or accelerated the adoption or rejection of the specific items of the Dance.

A regional study of culture elements where the overall identity of a culture is kept in view should be placed in this category of empiric aggregates. It is not altogether dissimilar to the 'culture area' approach. The interest here is in the distribution of culture elements and for this purpose the idea of culture centers in the area is utilized. List of traits is used to show "variations and culminations within certain aspects of culture" (Steward 1961:1056) and to find out similarities between the tribes of the region. Actual comparisons are made to note the presence and absence of the elements. Statistics may be used to show similarity between any two societies. A coefficient of correlation may be expressed on the basis of mutual presence and absence of traits. This was done by some members of Kroeber's team in the California Culture Element Survey.

In his *Cultural and Natural Areas of Native North America* (1939), Kroeber expanded the idea of cultural climax. It replaced somewhat simple assumptions of the concepts of culture center and marginal culture. The centers were more complex; so it was presumed that they were more inventive than the uninventive peripheries. The concept of cultural climax laid stress on cultural intensification rather than on the locus of inventiveness.

Comparison of Cultural Wholes

In any discussion of a comparative study of the cultural wholes certain questions should be answered first. What is a cultural whole? Is a total coverage of all its parts possible? A cultural whole may be a tribal, a folk, or a civilizational whole. Further, it is neither possible nor desirable to cover all the parts of a cultural whole. So the comparison of wholes poses problems of selection. There has to be somewhat different treatment of whatever traits, complexes or, even institutions are selected as representative of the whole.

Comparison of Tribal Wholes

One way to compare tribal wholes is through their respective configurations or spirits. In this case total culture patterns are translated into psychological characterizations which are supposed to represent deep-seated principles guiding the lives of the people of that culture. Benedict's *Patterns of Culture* (1934) is such a study. The comparisons are supposed to show differences, not similarities. Cultures differ more, says Benedict, because "they are oriented as wholes in different directions."

Comparison of Civilizational Wholes

Another way to study cultural wholes is to take note of the cultural content and emphasis rather than the configuration. The data are not interpreted in terms of psychological 'diagnoses' but in the light of diachronic generalized processes. To delimit civilizations as cultural wholes is a big challenge to anthropology.

The historian is concerned with the totality of historical events. To him civilizations are somewhat arbitrary, though meaningfully, segregated segments from the totality. In cultural terms, the anthropologist's delimitation of a civilizational whole cannot be in terms of a single unique characteristic. He is more concerned than the historian, with relatively enduring products and results of human behavior and acts than with events. Kroeber's *Configurations of Culture Growth* (1944) is a classic example — of both the weakness and the strength — of an anthropological approach to a holistic study. Kroeber, unlike Spengler, found that civilizations passed through peaks of cultural climaxes or culminations rather than the cycle of birth and death. He tells us that a student of culture can delimit or segregate one civilization from the other "partly by geography, partly by period; partly by speech, religion, government, less by technology; most of all, by those activities of civilization that are especially concerned with values and the manifest qualities of style" (1963:17).

Another study of a civilizational whole may face the above problem somewhat differently. The focus in this case may be on the problem. In this way the range from which the wholes can be chosen for comparison is delimited automatically. For instance, by concentrating on the emergence of new levels of organization connected with the development of early agriculture, Julian Steward did not have too many civilizations to deal with . . . Peru, Mesopotamia, Meso-America, Egypt and China were compared under such broad headings as technologies, transportation, social features, and intellectual traits (Steward 1955).

COMPARISON OF CONCEPTUAL AGGREGATES

A conceptual aggregate, unlike an empiric aggregate, is a collection of categories or ideas which may not be combined that way in reality even though the parts may be empirically referable. The aggregate is, then, a result of conceptualization and reconstruction by the anthropologist. In this class we shall deal with totemism and culture complexes *(Kulturkreise)*.

Comparison of Totemism as a Conceptual Aggregate

For several decades in the late nineteenth and the early twentieth centuries, totemism was a major topic of discussion among anthropologists. Totemism is a none-too-precisely defined conceptual category treated at times as if it were an institution. Goldenweiser once concluded that totemism was more a fiction than a fact. But at another time he also called it an institution: "Totemism is one of the most widespread *institutions* of primitive society. . . ." and ". . . an *institution* so general in primitive society. . . ." Further, "while the two *institutions* — totemism and religious societies — present, from a theoretical standpoint, a set of similar problems" (Goldenweiser 1931:363, 363 and 387; all emphases supplied).

Radcliffe-Brown asked once if 'totemism' as a technical term has not outlived its usefulness (1929 in 1952:117). Then he proceeded with his discourse by indicating the 'basic' features of 'totemism.' Lévi-Strauss's book on totemism (1963b) shows that interest in it is far from dead. Our main concern at present is to find which features (i.e., items) are covered in the different comparative studies of totemism.

Goldenweiser talks of a totemic complex. It is a list of all the features which form totemism. There is nothing intrinsically 'totemic' about them. It is not necessary that all these be present in all the totemic groups. In his substantive study of totemism Goldenweiser makes a detailed comparison of Australia and the Northwest coast of North America in regards to the 'symptoms' of totemism. Then, the same 'symptoms' form the basis to examine a wider and more heterogeneous material. The totemic 'symptoms' which form the totemic complex are the following: exogamy, totemic names, descent from the totem, number of totems, taboo, magical ceremonies, reincarnation of ancestral spirits, guardian spirit and secret society, art and rank. In Goldenweiser's view the analytical treatment of the totemic complex deprives it of all individuality in specific composition. It is so because "each and all of the characteristics of totemic complexes find their replicas outside of that content" (1933:345: originally published in 1919 under the title, "Form and Content in Totemism," in *American Anthropologist*).

If one casts off the contrasts, a core remains. The focal point of totemism is a sib system. The specific mechanisms through which different combinations of the totemic features came into being must have been varied. But with the historical (or historico-geographical) point of view the problem of totemism does not evaporate behind the problems of local totemic complexes. According to Goldenweiser's historical perspective the sib forms an important phase in the history of primitive institutions. Totemism regularly, though not invariably, accompanies this phase of primitive society. "Exogamy, a mystical man-nature relationship and functional homology of equivalent social units become associated in totemism by adopting a sib system as their carrier. And they adopt a sib system as their carrier because such a system is admirably fitted to become a vehicle for the crystallization and enhancement of these features" (1931:384).

By totemism Radcliffe-Brown means the division of a society into groups and a special relation (a ritual relation) between each group and the natural species of animals and plants. His study of totemism is distinctive for two reasons. Firstly, he does not systematically compare different totemic societies on the basis of the *elements* of totemism. Secondly, according to him, to understand totemism one has to tackle the wider and more general problem of the "relation between man and natural species in mythology and ritual" (1952:117). One has to look also for clues to totemism in nontotemic tribes such as the Andamanese and the Eskimo. In his main essay on totemism (1929) Radcliffe-Brown devised a formula which he believed accounted for the formalization of totemism from the general conception of the universe as a moral order. According to Radcliffe-Brown the conditions in which the universal element of culture is most likely to take the form of totemism are: "(1) dependence wholly or in part on natural productions for subsistence; and (2) the existence of a segmentary organization into clans and moieties or other similar social units" (1952:132). In a later essay, entitled "The Comparative Method in Social Anthropology" (1951), he compared certain aspects of myths among the tribes of Australia and North America. The interest here was to find out the principle of the pair of opposites and the resolution of opposition as depicted in the myths.

Lévi-Strauss agrees with those who hold that the term 'totemism' does not correspond to a real institution. The speculations of some very able minds of the last century about totemism, Lévi-Strauss tells us, were fruitless because the heart of the matter lay at a deeper level than the one they considered. The 'totemic illusion' was a projection by scholars beyond modern Western society, reaching out to the customs and beliefs which differed from the manner of thinking of an average white man. Lévi-Strauss attempts to show that there is no fundamental difference between the thinking of the 'totemic' and the 'nontotemic' people. Like Radcliffe-Brown he considers totemism a particular way of formulating a general human problem of the relation between man and nature. He also agrees with Radcliffe-Brown with the necessity of comparing different myths. The result is already established: totemism is a particular expression of "how to make opposition, instead of being an obstacle to integration, serve rather to produce it" (Lévi-Strauss 1963b:89).

All three anthropologists considered totemism difficult to specify. Goldenweiser later changed his view, associating totemism with clan in a special organizational set-up. All three scholars compared. Goldenweiser confined his comparisons to the 'totemic' societies only. Radcliffe-Brown thought he had to compare totemic with nontotemic tribes if a solution of the problem of totemism was to be found. Lévi-Strauss found it necessary to compare the idea systems of totemic and nontotemic (Western) societies. The three also differed in the level of abstraction and the closeness to the reality of the data. This consequently made a difference in what they actually compared.

Comparison of 'Cultural Complexes' as Conceptual Aggregates

A 'culture complex' is a collection or a grouping of culture elements or traits. The association of the traits poses a difficult conceptual problem. Herskovits says "the student, who is seeking a purely rational explanation of why certain elements found together should have been combined, is at times baffled by the apparent absence of logic in their conclusion" (1948:179 & 181). Yet to be meaningful, a certain degree of integration of the traits is necessary. One finds that sometimes a 'complex' used for comparison seems to be a mere agglomeration of traits.

Fritz Graebner's *Methode der Ethnologie* contains important methodological precepts of the German-Austrian (sometimes called the Vienna) Culture Historical School. *Kulturkreis* ('culture circle') and *Ferninterpretation* (interpretation of borrowing despite distance) are two basic tenets. A *Kreis* is a cultural type or a block of cultural material. It is not an *area* of culture. It is sometimes referred to as a culture-complex. Graebner's interest in cultures is to determine cultural connection and to establish "the temporal and causal relationship." That similarities between two cultures might arise as a consequence of independent parallel evolution, or of convergence, of originally distinct phenomena, is rejected by Graebner as inferior to his 'principle of historical connection.'

According to Graebner, culture-traits diffuse in "complexes, not in isolated elements." Lowie points out that "it is one of the cardinal doctrines of Graebner's philosophy of ethnology that the diffusion of isolated cultural elements — even myths — is impossible" (1912:25; 24). Migrations, which brought about the meeting of cultures, are traceable. The occurrence of complete or nearly complete identities between culture-complexes, even widely separated localities, is seen as the result of migration. Graebner describes six *Kulturkreise*. They are composed of unrelated elements. These utilize historical reconstruction as a goal. As a procedure the idea of accidental adhesions is stressed. Accidental adhesions become the criteria (i.e., the proof) of diffusion of a 'complex.' He postulates that these several 'culture circles' originated successively in time, and progressively in their degree of complexity. Each culture circle is said to have spread, more or less, over the whole world. It is represented in all cultures, although in varying mixed proportions. An important task of Graebnerian culture history was to compare the elements of any given culture to these *Kulturkreise* in order to determine their makeup. When a comparison of the elements of two or more cultures shows similarities, their derivation from a single source 'can' be worked out on how numerous (quantity) and how complex (form) the similarities are.

Robert von Heine-Geldern says that he rejected the *Kulturkreis* concept in its heyday. His paper, "Die asiatische Herkunft der sudamerikanischen Metalltechnik" is rated very highly in the Vienna circle. W. Koppers thought it "will prove a landmark in research on Old World and New World cultural relations and on the problem of diffusion in general" (1956:179). Let us examine it for its content. Heine-Geldern's comparison suggests to him similarities between some metal forms of the Caucasus and Hallstatt cultures, on the one hand, and some South American ones, on the other. It is farfetched to derive the latter from the former directly. So he postulates an intermediary Asian zone and a Pontic migration to the Far East, during a short period, followed by an eventual trans-Pacific migration. Many Caucasian metal forms found in South America are absent from the Far East. Several of them, although found in the Far East, are not found in the New World. Heine-Geldern assumes that the unknown forms are there in the Far East: "The lack of metal forms in the Far East comparable to those from the Caucasus and South America discussed in this paper does not mean anything. We can assume *mit guten Recht* that they are there and with further systematic investigation will be brought to light" (Heine-Geldern, 1954: quotations are from a 42-page English abstract prepared by Dr. P. Phillips of the Peabody Museum, Harvard University, pp. 3-4). In the Old World his metal forms come from a huge area extending from the Caucasus, on the one end, to Inner Mongolia, China, Indo-China and Indonesia, on the other. It is difficult to imagine any real unity for the complex. But he thinks it poses no problem because culture-historically they come from the same region. "These forms originally came from a single comparatively small region, the Caucasus" and so "however scattered they may appear, culture-historically they form a more or less closed complex" (Heine-Geldern, 1954:4). Thus Heine-Geldern's complex is similar, in its essentials, to Graebner's *Kulturkreis*. Both emerge from the comparison of 'complexes' of cultural elements which are not fully integrated.

SUMMARY AND CONCLUSIONS

Though not exhaustive, the content of this chapter gives us an idea of the units and the items compared. By a unit of comparison we mean the totality which is the point of reference for comparison with another totality of a similar nature. An item of comparison is that part of the unit which is actually compared. In the case of a comparison of culture traits the unit and the item may be the same. Whole cultures as units are usually compared through one or more items.

A trait is an independent unit of comparison. The problem of its definition can be solved only with reference to the context. A trait may be a biologic given, e.g., sex. It may be a material manifestation like pottery or basketry. It may be a set of rules in games, such as, Patolli and Pachisi. In one case it can be only a relationship like a mother's brother's relationship to his sister's son. A trait can be broken further but the parts do not remain minimal significant divisions of a culture in that context. An institution in its many forms is one of the most common units of comparison. We have seen that the items compared under the unit 'social organization' are varied.

Another class of units of comparison may be aggregates or combinations of categories. Communities, 'culture areas' and cultural wholes are the types of aggregates that can be empirically referred to. In intracultural comparisons two or more communities of the same culture are compared. When two communities at the same level of organization are chosen for comparison the result is different from a comparison of such units at different levels of organization. Fortes's Ashanti case study and Redfield's Yucatan folk culture study clearly demonstrate this difference.

Cultural wholes as units of comparison are represented through items. Something is always chosen to represent this big unit. The item may be a trait, a theme, an institution or a group, or a combination of one or more of these. When the cultural wholes compared are at the same scale, the problem of their delimitation becomes important only when one deals with civilizations. The historian treats a civilization as a segment of the totality of events; the anthropologist treats it as a cultural whole. Several categories like speech, religion, government, etc., besides geography and the time period, may be used for the purpose of defining a civilization as a cultural whole. In another case the choice of the problem may at the same time delimit the range of choice of the civilizational units and thus reduce the problem of definition to a minimum.

'Culture areas' are also empiric aggregates.

When an aggregate is chosen on the basis of the researcher's conceptualization rather than its being empirically referable, we shall call it a conceptual aggregate. Totemism is a notable example of a conceptual aggregate. For decades anthropologists have had a variety of ideas about it. A culture-complex, similarly, is an aggregate in which the combination of items is not always empirically referable and the conceptions of the researcher have a lot to do with its delineation in that form.

Purposes of Comparison

In the last chapter we discussed the categories used for comparisons. Now we shall deal with the purposes or goals of comparison. In other words, we shall try to find out what a researcher hopes to accomplish by comparing.

Broadly speaking, both scientific and historical goals can be attained through comparison (Radcliffe-Brown 1951:15). It may aim to show similarities or differences between phenomena as wholes, or of their parts or of their qualities. It is interesting to mention here the differences in emphasis on this point. Radcliffe-Brown holds that the purpose of comparison is to arrive at valid generalizations "by the systematic study of *resemblances and differences*" (1958:165; emphasis supplied).

In Evans-Pritchard's view the sociological purpose of a comparison is "to explain *differences rather than similarities*" (1963:16; emphasis supplied). He "would like to place emphasis on the importance for social anthropology as a comparative discipline of differences" (1963:17).

One researcher may wish to establish correlations through comparison, another may wish to demonstrate co-variation, and a third may seek causes. Some scholars may use a comparative approach to arrange or to classify things and to build typologies and to see variants from them. To infer 'historical' sequences and to show genetic relations may be the chosen purpose of yet another class of researchers. Generalizations of more or less universal validity, i.e., laws, are often attempted through comparison. Some aspire to formulate laws of 'development' or the generalized process. We can group all the different purposes for which comparisons are made under the following broad categories in the order given below, proceeding from the specific to the more general:

> Inferential history
> Typology
> Generalizations and laws
> Generalized process

INFERENTIAL HISTORY

A few words about history are a necessity in order to clarify what we mean by inferential history. History, it is believed, tells us what really happened. But in reality it is impossible for it to do so. A historian selects from amongst the historical material available to him and he adds to it his interpretation. All history is thus reconstruction. The time factor is an important feature of history, though not an essential one. Individuation, or preserving the quality of the phenomena, is a basic feature which distinguishes history from science. The former deals with specific items — persons, events, institutions, etc. — in a more or less well-demarcated universe. It is not possible to substantiate the findings of history by the proofs as in the natural sciences. A historian infers the probabilities of fact, of relation, of significance (cp. Kroeber 1952:79). He says further that a historian's business is "a judicial weighing of possibilities and a selection and combination of these into the most coherent whole or pattern."

History depends upon written documents or on archaeological findings for its data. It is possible that the historical evidence may be misused by a pseudo-historian. A pseudo-historian is one who decides upon a position he wants to justify, and manipulates the evidence to support his position. What will happen when there is no reliable evidence of a historical nature? In such cases imagination will run wild.

Anthropology differs from history in an important respect. In it there are few, if any, sequences of events. The anthropologist's conventional objects of study are primitive cultures in which there are no recorded events save the ones contained in the anthropologist's field notes. There are no verifiable events either. As a consequence, the anthropologist deals with structures and patterns (cp. Kroeber 1952:75). Some anthropologists tried to infer time elements from the spatial distributions of the cultural elements. This could not be called history in the proper sense of the word. In inferential history the origin or development of a trait or a complex, an institution or a community is hypothesized on the basis of knowledge of its present condition and in default of historical evidence. Inferential history uses 'theories' (like evolution) or facts of distribution to reconstruct time sequences. It is an attempt to write history without any historical data worth the name. Kroeber points out that a reasonably authentic and organized history is impossible without written documents (1954:279). Now we shall briefly analyze some attempts of anthropologists to do inferential history through a comparative method.

Inferential history is of two types. Developmental sequences, supposed to be applicable to all societies, were very popular with the 'classical' evolutionists and with some diffusionists as well. Distribution-based sequences of traits or trait-complexes in limited regional compass were usually the work of the Americanists.

Tylor's comparative study of marriage and descent had been undertaken for two purposes. One of them, which concerns us here, was inferential history. He favored 'speculative explanation' (Tylor's phrase). By his 'social arithmetic' (i.e., by tabulation and classification), he would disclose 'social history,' which in this case was the development of institutions. An axiom of his inferential history is that the human institutions are as much stratified as the earth which man lives upon. From evolutionary 'principles' he assumed that invariably all societies have passed from the maternal institutions to the paternal ones. A natural corollary to this 'rule' should be that all existing matrilocal societies must be the more primitive. When it was found not to be true in all cases, the evolutionists had a loophole in the principle of 'survivals.'

The Patolli-Pachisi relation problem clearly shows that Tylor was open to account for 'origins' in terms of diffusion in the heyday of unilinear evolution. In this case his inferential historical derivations are buttressed with probability statistics. As we indicated earlier, he divided the two games into items to compare them. "The more numerous are such elements," says Tylor, "the more improbable the recurrence of their combination" (Tylor 1896:66). Since in Tylor's view there is a sixth order recurrence of the combination, the relation between Patolli and Pachisi can be accounted for only by diffusion before the Spanish conquest of the New World. In 1931 Kroeber considered that there was a real homology between Patolli and Pachisi, and thus a genetic unity was evident. But in his *Anthropology* (1948), he considers the question of relation still open. He accepts Tylor's argument on the basis of similarity in the elements (items) of the two games. But he himself now throws cold water on the genetic relationship between the two games because the other things which might have migrated from the Old World to the New World have not survived with Patolli in any identifiable form.

How comparison can be used to infer 'history' from nonhistorical facts can be seen in Heine-Geldern's study of some South American metal forms. The goal is to show that some South American metallurgy originated in Asia. A comparison revealed similarities between the Caucasian and Hallstatt metal forms and those of South America. So the first inferred 'historical' suggestion is a rapid Pontic migration from Europe to East and Southeast Asia. When some Caucasian forms found in South America are absent in the Asian Zone, their presence is assumed. The inferred 'history' tells us that they are there and will be found when more is known about the Dong-Son culture of Southeast Asia. Moreover, the important fact of change in form through diffusion is altogether circumvented.

A more rigorously factual, nevertheless inferential, history is to be found in some studies of culture-traits and culture-complexes. Klimek (1939) studied the origins of the different Californian Indian cultures and attempted their 'stratification.' The groups of tribes which have similar inventories constitute cultural provinces. The groups of culture elements which have a similar distribution form a cultural stratum. Every cultural stratum is linked to a definite ethnic group. The cultures are built up through the processes of contact, migration, and differentiation. But the knowledge of ethnic connection will allow one to establish the historical nature of the strata. With these guidelines in mind, Klimek postulated that the lowest stratum of the California Indian culture is formed by Hokan and Yuki groups. Penutian came next and they in turn were followed by Shoshonean or Athabascan-Algonkin expansions. This is as good an imaginative construct as any other. There is no definite chronological reference point on which Klimek could base his reconstructions.

From a detailed comparative study of the different elements which make up the Sun-Dance complex Leslie Spier concludes that the essentials of the ceremony are everywhere the same. His professed goal is 'historical,' i.e., to trace the relations between the various Sun-Dance ceremonies. It is done in a general way rather than by tracing how and when the elements of the dance were transmitted. He is concerned with the psychological factors involved in the transmission, modification, acceptance, or rejection of the elements of the Sun Dance. He marks out the essential feature of the ceremony by ascertaining the center of a class of traits. His argument, in its essentials, is that of inferential history. Erecting a pole within an encircling structure is considered the essential core, and thus the original nucleus of the Sun Dance. The torture is of secondary importance and was included later. On these lines the historical position of the dance among the tribes concerned 'can' be inferred. The fact of acquisition through diffusion eliminates those tribes which seem to have acquired the important features recently.

In historical 'explanation' attempts are made, Eggan tells us, "to work out the sequences of events which lead to a certain end result" (1950:7). But it is only inferential history, not history, to say that the Zuñi once had an operating dual division in the past because their mythology suggests so. They do not have it today, we are told, because it was cumbersome and had to be eliminated. Further, the intermediate position of the Keresan-speaking Ácoma and Laguna villages between the Hopi and the Zuñi on the one hand, and the Tiwa and Tewa, on the other, is accounted for in this way. All Keresan social organization was originally of the western Pueblo type. Along with the other eastern Pueblos, the Keresan changed to the eastern type. Then, again, under acculturative influences Ácoma and Laguna villages changed into the present western Pueblo variety. This is an example of imaginative 'historical' reconstruction. Eggan has done some surprising speculation. The eastern Pueblo Tiwa and Tewa do not have a clan system. He accepts the possibility that they may never have had it. But he goes on to imagine that they had it in the past. After having done this, Eggan has now to get rid of the imaginary clan system by means of, to use his own words, "a very complicated historical hypothesis." He justifies all this speculation by pointing out that the history of the Pueblos has been complex and it needs a correspondingly complex statement (1950:318).

TYPOLOGY

The making of typologies is an acknowledged goal of comparisons. Some anthropologists consider typology-building to be the exclusive task of comparison. A more moderate view is expressed by Raymond Firth. He says that "the essence of the comparative method in social anthropology" is that the comparison is made "with the object of establishing types and seeking variants from them" (1951:18). Leach takes an extreme position in his *Rethinking Anthropology* (1961b) when he denounces typology-building as 'butterfly collecting.' He rejects comparison because, in his view, its outcome is typology. It seems he does not think generalization can be obtained through com-

parison. He would, otherwise, not set up generalization as an alternative to comparison. This point will be discussed further in some detail
later. At first we shall examine what is meant by a type.

The archaeologist's use of the type concept is determined by the
material of his study. He digs up artifacts. The trait-index attracts
his attention immediately. The historical relevance of the units is also
considered a necessary factor in the definition of a type by several
New World archaeologists, such as Rouse (1939), Krieger (1944),
Spaulding (1953), and Ford (1954). If we accept this emphasis of
the archaeologists, much work by social-cultural anthropologists cannot
be called typologizing.

In social-cultural anthropology the phenomena are usually quali-
tatively conceived. This is a prerequisite even of the quantification of
features. The synchronic treatment of the material is also very common.
So any workable definition of a type should not exclude these facts.
A *type* is a group of manifestations, representing the modal tendency
of a class of phenomena, which have enough common features to be
put together and are distinguishable from another group of manifestations. Thus, both similarities and differences are important in typology.
A type may be directly referable to empirical reality. It may be based
on a reconstruction of reality. An ideal type of Max Weber's falls in
this category. We follow Howard Becker in calling it a reconstructed
type.

Types can be grouped in various ways. A descriptive-analytical
typology is concerned with synchronic facts and is based on contextual
comparison. It is closer to phenomenal reality. A morphological
(formal) type and a functional type fall into this category. A reconstructed type may be either of the two. The other broad class is that
of the historical-developmental typology. Diachronic facts are grouped
in this class. The historical-index and the total-culture types are the
main subdivisions.

Culture-traits, either individually or in a group, readily serve as
the criteria, indicators, or markers of a type. They are concrete items.
A list of traits may be used to find out the common and the uncommon
aspects of a group of cultures. Culture areas may be the outcome of
such efforts. Kroeber's and Klimek's most substantive result of the
culture element study was a sharper definition of the culture areas of
California tribes. A culture area is not a type. It is an attempt, no
doubt, to distinguish a whole from another whole. But it is neither
based on an idea nor on a typical institution which shows integrative
features. Klimek's 'historical' conclusions may seem similar to an

archaeologist's reconstruction. But we have indicated earlier that his strata are not historical-index types of the archaeologist. However abused, Graebner's *Kulturkreis* ('culture circle') concept seems closer than a culture area to a type concept. It does not have a real dimension built into it because it is only a block of cultural material. As is well known, the *Kulturkreise* were considered indicators of historical growth of cultures. They were also thought to be quite homogeneous. None of the claims was fully substantiated by empiric demonstrations. A *Kulturkreis* was neither an integrated whole of traits close to reality nor was it a reconstructed type.

It is not uncommon to build typologies after an institution, a group, or a set of relations. L. H. Morgan's descriptive and classificatory types of kinship system are well-known. McLennan's matrilineal and patrilineal types are equally celebrated. Both these typologies were based on morphological features, but were used as historical-index types. For evolutionary developmental sequences one of the two things was needed. If the types were sharply defined, some sort of stratified succession of these was essential. Tylor postulated that "the institutions of man are as distinctly stratified as the earth on which he lives" (1895:269). An intermediary type indicating transition between the two extremes was the other alternative. Tylor's detailed comparative work resulted in a modified version of McLennan's original typology — matrilineal, matri-patrilineal, and patrilineal.

Comparative studies for the purpose of building typologies may be done with different aims. Lowie and Radcliffe-Brown compared extensively. Their interest was not to justify the evolutionary sequence from one type (state) to the other. The morphological (formal) analysis of the existing examples of the types demonstrated the essentially bilateral character of the so-called unilateral systems. This also rendered obsolete the idea of matriarchate and patriarchate, as conceived by the nineteenth-century anthropologists. The studies of contemporary anthropologists further extend Lowie's and Radcliffe-Brown's work by examining the degree of matrilateral ties and typing them as patri-matrilateral and matri-matrilateral, etc. (Goody 1959:67). The focus has shifted to the morphological (formal) — functional type in the broad descriptive and analytical category.

In unilinearity the major interest centers around the descent groups. The study of kinship terminology for typology-building has also survived. But an important problem is that of the isolability of an institution for comparison. The same institution may be found in societies which are not at the same level of development in terms of their means of subsistence and other economic features. Murdock is in this dilemma.

He bases his typology on a single aspect of kinship terminology (that is, on cousin terms) (Murdock 1949). One way to avoid this shortcoming is to base types on more than one criterion. In the case of descent groups, besides descent, the criteria of corporateness, unilinearity, stratification, and ranking are used by Morton Fried. He comes out with eight basic types: Egalitarian clan, Ranking clan, Stratified clan, Ranking and Stratified clan; Egalitarian lineage, Ranking lineage, Stratified lineage, Ranking and Stratified lineage (1957:24). This attempt does not answer the question, posed earlier, about the correlation of institutions and cultures. Fried is fully aware of this problem (1957:1). But when the question of classification comes, he skirts the problem of correlation by saying that he was "not talking about societies but about corporate unilinear descent groups" (1957:24).

Leach has criticized typology-construction very strongly in his first Malinowski lecture (1961b:283). One would hesitate to associate him with any such act. Nevertheless one finds at least two typologies in his writings both belonging in our descriptive-analytical category. The first, a more descriptive one, is about marriage. One of the major types is that of 'private (individual) marriage.' The other type is an institutionalized or 'type' marriage. This is further divisible in Kariera, Trobriand, and Kachin subtypes on the basis of symmetrical or asymmetrical cross-cousin marriage (1961b:56 & 59). His *gumsa* and *gumlao* types are more analytical. They are two reconstructed types of a political system. They represent two poles between which a mixed type is formed from time to time. They are not permanent or stable organizations. Their isolability depends on an anthropologist's reconstruction. Lehman, who confirms Leach's views, supports our contention. He says that "the rules for getting from one state to another are, *as it were,* built into the general culture permanently" (1964:389; italics supplied).

To represent whole cultures by certain basic ideas, themes or spirits demands a high degree of abstraction and reconstruction. Cultures use only a segment of the great arc of potential human purposes and motivations, said Ruth Benedict. In spite of her objection to labeling Apollonian and Dionysian as types (cp. Benedict 1934:238), they were really nothing else. They are polar opposites and are formal-functional types in which a broad descriptive-analytical focus is retained.

Typologies built to show growth and development of communities or even of whole cultures have altogether different dimensions. They may or may not be polar types. If they are polar types the passage from one to the other is not obvious. Redfield's idea of the transformation from a primitive state to a civilized state brings out the point quite clearly. He works at a very high level of abstraction so that the difference between the contemporary primitives and the prehistoric preliterates is not found significant. It would be difficult to do so and to take as indicators of all the primitive cultures (past and present) any tangible aspects. The chosen characteristics are 'abstractions' such as the predominance of moral order, homogeneity, isolation, etc. The comparison shows that the change or transformation is to be seen in the change towards the opposite of the above-mentioned characteristics in various degrees and in different combinations thereof. Redfield's typology is highly reconstructed.

Less abstract and closer to the historical fact, though still based on reconstruction, may be a typology based on an easily definable and located part of a culture.

A cultural type is not based on one or more psychological characteristics. It may be an analytical one. Integration of form as well as of function is emphasized by some (Steward 1955). Such a typology may be built to arrive at 'causal' relations. Comparisons between cultures from far and wide may also be attempted. The differences are to be noted as well as the similarities. The apparent dissimilarities in the environments and the natural resources of the Congo Negrito, Bushman, Australians, Tasmanians, Philippine Negritos, Semang, Patagonian Tehuelche, Southern California Shoshones did not dissuade Steward from seeking the underlying regularity in terms of 'causal' relations. These various environmental conditions posed similar problems to sparse human populations which gave rise to patrilineal bands in all these communities. Steward (1955) says that "when similar form and function develop independently they may be classed in a single cultural type."

The urge to seek causal formulae may lead to developmental typologies as well. The concept of 'cultural core' refers to a set of features functionally interrelated which have diagnostic value for a developmental typology. Steward's irrigational civilization is an example. The problem in this case is to find what conditions were associated with the emergence of early agricultural civilizations of both the Old World and the New World. In spite of the difference in time the stages through which these civilizations pass are found to be similar.

GENERALIZATION AND LAWS

The question of history and/or science in anthropology has been a hot issue for the last few decades. The disputants often take extreme positions. Attempts have been made to show that the 'scientific' and the 'historical' approaches in anthropology are incompatible, or even diametrically opposed. A proper appraisal of the rival claims becomes difficult because the key words are only imprecisely defined or are not defined at all. Moreover, we are only concerned here with the implications the controversy may have for comparative study in social-cultural anthropology.

That facts of social-cultural anthropology are 'historically determined' does not mean that they are historical facts. It is true that the anthropologist works among a particular people in a fixed time and space. His data are not oriented towards events as those of history normally are. His account is a generalized picture of a particular community illustrated with particular examples, but not in a chronological order. Evans-Pritchard believes that the subject-matter of social anthropology imposes restrictions upon its scientific treatment. He indicates social anthropology's closeness to history by asking whether it is not itself a kind of historiography (1950; reprinted in 1964.148). In a reconsideration of this issue, Evans-Pritchard admits that even for investigating the same problem the anthropologist and the historian would not take the same facts for their data and they would not obtain them in the same manner.

To define a discipline by the kind of data it studies would mean that geology, astronomy and, in parts, biology are historical rather than scientific disciplines. It is true that the nature of the social-cultural phenomena limits somewhat the expanse of the scientific nature of social-cultural anthropology. But there is no valid reason to deny that regularities can be discovered behind the specificity of the particular facts. If we were to follow Carl G. Hempel this problem would not even arise. According to him the historical explanation is not different from the scientific one. Both are deductive and are based on general covering laws. Historians and many philosophers also do not accept Hempel's covering law model explanation. But it raises a very important issue — that of regularities, generalizations or laws.

A hypothesis may arise in a dream, in imagination, in an intuition or in some concrete experience. Usually a scientist combines shrewd guess and scientific intuition with careful observation to arrive at a set of postulates which covers the phenomena he is interested in. A *hypothesis* is a statement the consequences derived from which must be testable by experience. To be effective, a hypothesis must be capable of deductive development (cp. Alexander 1963:107) and empirical verification.

A *generalization* is defined as a principle which asserts some attribute about all or some of the members of a class of objects (cp. Black 1952:281). One point is missing from this otherwise excellent definition of a generalization. All general statements are not generalizations. A generalization is obtained in only one way. That way is by arguing from a particular instance to 'all' the instances of the same kind. Alexander (1963:105) says that "calling a statement 'general' is saying something about the range of its applicability, whereas calling it a 'generalization' is also saying something about how it was reached." In a uniform generalization all the members of a class are represented. A statistical generalization represents most (or such-and-such a portion) of a class of phenomena.

Many social scientists — and most social-cultural anthropologists — are alarmed when their colleagues talk of social 'laws.' This alarm stems from a belief that a law is a regularity or a principle which is unalterable once it is established. In fact a law is only a generalization with the universal schema, "all A is B" or "for any x, if x is A, then x is B." A law has a field. Its content is determined by its context. All crows are black tells us that "any individual thing which happens to exist whether in the past, present or future and which satisfies the condition for being a crow is in point of fact also black" (Nagel 1961:50). Thus a *law* is a universal conditional which formulates a 'constant conjunction' of traits (crow and black). It asserts only matter-of-fact connections and expresses *de facto* universality.

Comparison can be used to accomplish various tasks. The anthropologist's almost exclusive concern with a single people at a certain period of their existence is a hindrance to comparison. The categories under which a culture is to be described or cultures are to be compared are themselves established through comparison. The 'classical' anthropologist's categories were built with a special purpose in view. Comparative studies in the first two decades of the present century were undertaken to establish new categories and to expand those already established. Malinowski's *The Family* did two things on the basis of comparison. It conclusively demolished the fiction that the most 'primitive' Australian aborigines did not have elementary family. It also presented the format for any comparative study of the family. Lowie's comparative studies showed that the so-called matrilineal complex had no real existence and the unilineal systems had important bilateral features. His effort also included a redefinition of categories like sib, association, property, etc., which were dealt with previously. But to discuss primitive societies in terms of rank, government, and justice was bold and imaginative, in his day. It is obvious that Lowie had formulated his categories before he actually compared. They were intuitively and unsystematically arrived at on the basis of wide ethnographic reading.

An attempt somewhat limited, both in area and in subject-matter, was Radcliffe-Brown's clarification of the operational categories like 'cycle,' 'pair,' 'couple,' etc., with regard to the Kariera system. A more recent attempt to re-examine the conceptual unit categories used by anthropologists to describe and analyze kinship organization is found in Murdock's *Social Structure.* It contains redefinition of terms like clan, avuncular, neo-local, deme, etc. Still more recently Morton Fried his tried to define more precisely the corporate unilineal descent group and did that through comparison.

When we talk of causation we mean normally that a certain antecedent "C" is followed by a consequent "E" under specified conditions. We imply here a generalization about any happenings of the same kind. But all generalizations do not, and need not, refer to causes. An interesting and pertinent example of this is the general statement that swamps and mosquitos occur together. But it cannot be concluded that the one is the cause of the other (cp. Black 1952:323). A conjunction, or correlation, of features is usually the best we have, in social-cultural anthropology, in the name of a generalization.

Our general comprehension of the family is not improved when we are told (by Smith) that marriage does not exhaust mating and the mating organization 'explains' the family system (1962:255; 265). This does not imply that the information on mating and family, about particular communities, is not of any value. But such general statements do not yield worthwhile porpositions. Similarly, to say that there are correlations between marriage type, residential grouping, and economic and political organization is common knowledge (Richards 1950:251). It does not add anything significant to the body of existing anthropological knowledge. It is not useless but it would be better if we were told how a certain feature was related with certain other feature(s) in a definite way and how this relationship changed if certain changes in one of the features occurred.

Kinship has attracted much attention. A well-known formulation is sometimes called the extension of sentiment hypothesis. It was first called the principle of the equivalence of brothers, that of siblings and the unity of the sibling group. The ego expects care and indulgence from the mother. This relation to the mother is "generalized and extended to the kindred" (Radcliffe-Brown 1952:25). The fact that this statement is not true in all cases is beside the point. It is general but is not precise enough to be called a law. A critic of this formulation does not do any better when he says that "the relationship of a man with his father will be more full of tension in a patrilineal system than in a matrilineal one . . ." (Goody 1959:85). The use of the word tension introduces vagueness. These two formulations only indicate assumption of correlation between some factors.

Some statements about marriage rules which gave rise to much discussion regarding the definition of marriage may seem to be more tightly formulated. But a close scrutiny shows something else. We are told by Gluckman that "divorce rate is only one index of the general durability of marriage which is a function of the kinship structure as a whole" (1950:190). The first part of this statement, in the form presented by the author, is so obvious that no elaborate comparative study is needed to confirm it. It would be a different story if 'durability' was properly defined and a precise relationship between it and the rate of divorce was indicated. The second part simply says that there is some correlation(?) ('functional' relation) between the kinship structure and the durability of marriage, but we are not told what these are. It does not enhance our knowledge much because the amount of goods transferred (as bridewealth) and the divorce rate are also said to be "rooted in the kinship structure" (Gluckman 1950:192).

Our criticism is not that there are several correlations. It is recognized that the methods of elimination are not suitable for the type of social studies anthropologists conduct. It is also true that simple one-to-one correlations are not possible. The concomitant variations study may result in multiple types of interdependence and more than one concomitant. Nadel's comparative study of the role of witchcraft in four African societies is a balanced methodological attempt. It tested the hypotheses and assumptions concerning relations between witchcraft and tensions and anxieties. But the results are correlations and not laws.

Lowie was a scholar whose main interest was in establishing typologies and in demolishing unilinear evolutionary hypotheses. But from his material useful universal generalizations can be formulated. He deserves credit for it. Two examples of such generalizations are given below:

(1)   In all human societies the family (comprised of a married couple and their children) is present as a basic institution. As a kingroup the family is bilateral. The rules of residence — patrilocal or matrilocal — affect the bilateral symmetry of the family relations by stressing one side only.

(2) In all human societies sexual restrictions always go hand in hand with the corresponding social restrictions. In any human society the privileged, or, licensed, familiarity between the persons of the opposite sex is socially sanctioned only if they are potential mates.

Totemism has been studied comparatively. We saw, in the last chapter, how it was difficult to deal with it as an institution because it really was an abstraction. Both Goldenweiser and Radcliffe-Brown have, one time or another, said so. In his final synthesis on this problem Goldenweiser made sib the carrier of totemism. The other diagnostic features of totemism which, he thought, prospered (1931:380) in a sib system were exogamy, a mystical man-nature relationship and a set of equivalent and functionally homologous social units. That these features were not only totemic was acknowledged (1931:380). Some sort of pattern had to be woven around these features with sib system as the focal point. But nothing like a law came out of the very scholarly study by Goldenweiser. In the degree of abstraction he did not rise above the level of the phenomena.

Radcliffe-Brown's sociological 'theory' of totemism was an attempt to treat the totemic problem in terms of something more general without forgetting the specificity. In 1929 he posed the problem in this form: "Can we show that totemism is a special form of a phenomenon which is universal in human society and is therefore present in different forms in all cultures?" (Radcliffe-Brown 1952:123). His general formulation approached the totemic problem at a higher level of abstraction. He saw it as a special form of "the general relation between man and natural species in mythology and ritual" (1952:132).

In all human societies there is some relationship between man and natural species. In totemic societies the totem is a natural species and becomes the object of ritual relation. Totemism is found only in the societies which are dependent wholly or in part on natural production for subsistence and have a segmentary organization into clans and moities or similar social units.

The problem of totemism can be dealt with at a still higher level of abstraction. In this case the problem is transferred from the level of segmentary organizations to myths and rituals. This is justified in the name that totemism is an abstraction rather than an institution. The contents of the myths are analyzed to find principles which apply to both totemic and nontotemic societies with regard to man-nature relationship. The idea of opposition strikes Lévi-Strauss as being distinctive. So the problem of totemism is seen as that of the reconciliation of opposition. We do not object to Lévi-Strauss seeking abstract principles so far removed from the subject-matter. But we feel that nothing substantial is accomplished when such vague generalities are presented and no attempt is made to link them with the specific problem or phenomenon — in the present case, totemism — which was there to start with.

GENERALIZED PROCESS

The term process is used both in anthropology and sociology. Nowhere is it precisely defined. By some sociologists the social process is social interaction and thus is an essential background for any social activity. Others who talk of social processes consider them only specific forms of interaction. There are certain socio-psychological trends, tendencies, or mechanisms — such as cooperation, competition, assimilation, etc. — which cannot be called groups or institutions. These are often called processes by sociologists as well as by anthropologists.

Without calling in question these and other usages of the term, the definition of a process should convey more dynamic meaning than is indicated above. To us a *process* means a movement, slow or rapid. It indicates a transition, in time, from one condition to the other. In order to distinguish our usage from that of others we shall call it a *generalized process*.

A generalized process can be arrived at in at least two different ways. In the first case the specificities of a particular socio-cultural system are involved. The nature of the study remains essentially synchronic. A restudy of a culture, when made by the same scholar, does involve depiction of movement from the first state of the culture to the second. It is an example of a generalized synchronic process inferred through dual-synchronic field studies. Such a restudy may have both specific and general implications.

Two small-scale societies (Tikopia and Chan Kom) are restudied. Both are isolated, one because it dwells on an island, the other because it did not want to participate in the activities of the surrounding communities and so created a sort of a barrier around it. When first studied, both used the native tongues, had limited wants which could be locally satisfied, had a religion already established and firmly rooted, and an economic system that had not much to do with money.

Both the communities changed — in some ways along similar lines, in others in different directions. In the case of the island community of Tikopia the change came through contact of a section of the population with aliens, due to internal movements and change from native faith to Christianity. In the other case (Chan Kom) the change came because the people decided they wanted a change; they set up a goal and set out to attain that. The change from one Christian faith to the other helped because they already possessed the spirit of the new faith. Redfield says that "these villagers had much of the Protestant ethic before they ever heard of the Protestantism" (1950:157). In both societies the fundamental social institutions did not change. The structure of ideals in both the societies remained essentially what they were when studied for the first time. But the expectations of both changed. Both reached a stage when they were ready for entering into a new phase. To borrow Firth's terminology, though the changes are essentially organizational in nature they are, nevertheless, significant enough to usher societies into the era of a structural change. The two would have different courses because of their geographical location and their relation to other communities of the same and/or different scale. These studies give us an interesting idea of the generalized process of organizational change.

The generalized diachronic process may take two forms. Both result from intensive comparison and in both a long time element is involved. One of these has a developmental-sequential order which is nonreversible. Julian Steward believes that the regularities in temporal perspective are possible. He is fond of cause-and-effect relationships. First of all cause-effect type of regularity is only one type and is not necessarily the best one. Moreover, as Steward's work shows the antecedent is more suitable for a synchronic rather than a diachronic study.

In a study of sequential order one needs some stage- or sequence-markers. Morgan used technological markers for his eras. Childe gave an economic twist to the markers, particularly to those of the 'revolutions.' Steward's distinctiveness lies in taking emergence of the new levels of organization as his chief criterion of the eras which are Preagricultural; Incipient Agriculture; Formative Era of Basic Technologies and Folk Culture; Era of Regional Development and Florescent States and Multi-state Empires based on conquest. This generalized process is limited to the so-called irrigation civilizations which flourished in the historical past in an arid environment. The latter may have played same part in similar developments in different areas of the world. But to stress ecological determinism would be naive. This formulation, based on historical data, could be possible because the researcher rose above the level of specificities and isolated critical aspects for a generalized treatment. In this sense it was a scientific approach, not a historical one.

At a higher level of abstraction one can deal with systems of ideas and organizations rather than with specific cultures or civilizations. Redfield's study of transformations from folk to urban, from village to city, and from moral order to technical order, from organization to disorganization to reorganization, from homogeneity to heterogeneity is an interesting example. In his studies Redfield did not suggest a literal movement from one state to the other — say, from moral to technical order. He considered them two different, but possibly related, frames of reference. All such studies need not necessarily be diachronic, as his own *Folk-Culture of Yucatan* demonstrates. But they may be so. This is apparent from his *Transformations* and "The Cultural Role of Cities."

There have been some attempts to formulate regularities of history. Spengler, Toynbee, and Sorokin are well-known for their attempts in this direction. Among the anthropologists Kroeber alone made efforts on such a large scale. He used anthropological concepts and methods on basically historical data to answer questions not normally posed by anthropologists. His attempt is distinctive because of his rigorous methodology — he followed a thoroughgoing inductive procedure. If he did not come up with spectacular generalizations it was not due to his inductive procedure. There were other reasons which we shall mention shortly. He also showed great intellectual balance in his descriptions and conclusions.

What did Kroeber want to know? First, he wanted to find out if there was any similarity in the configurations found in different regions and in different historical periods. There is sufficient variety among the civilizations. So it is not possible to say that their growth is "typically expressible by symmetrical normal curve" (Kroeber 1944: 841-42). Secondly, are the configurations of growth in one aspect of culture, e.g. mathematics, like those in the other aspects? There are both similarities and differences in this case. Thirdly to what extent do the several patterns of one culture form, culminate, and dissolve at the same time? (Kroeber 1944:822). In spite of some variations the different aspects of a culture seem to grow, climax, and atrophy more or less together.

These conclusions may not seem bold. Kroeber himself would not call them laws, far from it. In Clyde Kluckhohn's view the greatest weakness of Kreober's book is "a certain conceptual timidity" (1946: 340). Why is it so? It is not, as Leslie White thinks (cp. 1946:80), because Kroeber dealt with the aspects of a culture rather than the whole! It is obvious that Kroeber never forgot the wholeness. He wanted to see if there was any pattern detectable in the growth of the commonly accepted aspects of a culture. Moreover, he did not want to represent great civilizations through a single integrative idea. That is what he would have to do if he compared 'whole' cultures.

Kroeber's view of history affected his conclusions. He always stressed synthesis and the individuation of the data. He never wanted to outstrip the data of their specificity. So his approach to growth-configuration resulted in "a multiplicity of historic findings" rather than in universal diachronic laws. His real interest, it seems to us, was not in the configurations of culture growth as such. He wanted to make culture in its larger aspects of civilizational context intelligible. The primacy of culture concept did not leave any prominent place for the geniuses though they were considered important. In a sense Kroeber was testing the "great man" hypothesis.

SUMMARY AND CONCLUSIONS

All history is reconstruction of some sort. In inferential history, 'theories' (like evolution) and facts like distribution of culture elements may be used to reconstruct time sequences. The origin or development of a trait, a complex, an institution, or a community is hypothesized on the basis of knowledge of its present condition.

The examination showed that traits and complexes of traits are the most common items compared for inferential history, probably, because they are easily isolable and manipulable. Eggan's attempt to infer 'history' from the available Pueblo material is an exception. He postulated the presence and, then, subsequent loss of certain institutions and thus 'traced the history' of some aspects of the Pueblo cultures.

The nonmaterial elements are not commonly used in comparative studies yielding inferential history. Spier's Sun-Dance complex had both material and nonmaterial traits in it. We have also shown how the efforts of Heine-Geldern, Klimek, Kroeber, Tylor, etc. produce or do not produce inferential history.

Another goal or comparison may be typology-building. The archae-ologist's type concept is too limited to be of much use to the social-cultural anthropologist. A type is a group of manifestations representing the modal tendency of a class of phenomena. Both similarities and differences are important. A type may refer to the empirical reality directly or it may be a reconstruction based on the reality. An ideal type is a reconstructed type. Leach and Redfield have worked with reconstructed types.

A broad typological category is that of descriptive-analytical types. A morphological (or formal) type and a functional type fall in this broad category. The other comprehensive category is that of historical-developmental typology. Unlike the former it is diachronic in character. The historical-index and whole-culture types are its two main subdivisions.

A third aim of comparison may be generalization. The facts of social-cultural anthropology are historically determined but they are not facts of history. Though uncommon in anthropology, it is not impossible to arrive at a generalization in the sense of an empirically-arrived-at universal proposition about a class of social phenomena. Richard's and Gluckman's formulations, besides being commonplace, are not propositions precise enough to be called generalizations. Lévi-Strauss' pronouncements, on the other hand, are too abstract and vague. Lowie's and Radcliffe-Brown's statements, though not very precise, can be worked into some workable generalizations.

A generalized process may be the fourth goal of a comparison. It indicates movement in time from one state to a different one. A synchronic generalized process is obtainable through empirical restudies. Examples of such studies are provided by Redfield and Firth. They tell us how a generation of change, through internal and external factors, in a traditional society results in organizational or structural readjustments. A diachronic generalized process refers to the long-term changes or developments. The anthropologist uses historical material for such a study. Steward's study found a pattern of development in the social organization of the so-called irrigation civilizations of the Old World and the New World. Kroeber took whole civilizations for his comparative study. He did not discover any broad outline in the configuration(s) of their growth.

CHAPTER 4

Techniques and Methods of Comparison

We previously pointed out, in Chapter 1, that a technique should not be confused with a method. In this chapter we shall analyze techniques and methods of comparison. Techniques are quite important in the prosecution of research. But they are only the means to an end. The conceptualization of the problem determines the solution sought, and it also has a bearing on the choice of techniques which could accomplish the task. There is a close relation between the procedure and the purpose of a comparison. But we shall see that the same technique may be used to serve more than one purpose.

There are four aspects of any comparative method. They are: (1) technique(s); (2) goals (or purposes); (3) areal coverage of the material; and (4) unit(s) of comparison. In an ideal condition all four aspects may be neatly correlated. In our study we find that the two aspects which seem to go together are the technique of comparison and the areal coverage of the material. The picture becomes fuzzy if the remaining two are also combined. So, on the basis of the two correlated aspects there are three basic comparative methods in social-cultural anthropology:

(1) Illustrative Comparison (or Casual Comparison by Illustration)
(2) (Systematic) Complete-universe Comparison by Delimitation or (Areally Delimited Comparison)
(3) Hologeistic Comparison by Statistical Sampling or (Global Statistically Sampled Comparison)

ILLUSTRATIVE COMPARISON

The term 'illustrative comparison' has been used by Howard Becker (1940) for the approach of the nineteenth-century 'classical' anthro-

53

pologists. He contrasts his 'genuine comparison,' based on reconstructed types, from merely illustrative comparisons of these early anthropologists. Becker and Barnes (1938, I:760-61) had earlier outlined their view of "a genuinely comparative method" by introducing the idea of a reconstructed type. I do not agree with Becker that there is only one 'genuine' comparative method.

I shall ascribe the term 'illustrative' or 'casual' comparison to a group of scholars, besides the 'classical' anthropologists, who seem to share a common characteristic. They all compare casually or unsystematically. The technique utilized is that of illustration. Though quite common, the method of illustrative (casual) comparison is not generally recognized by anthropologists as a major comparative method. A few examples of the use of this method, which follow, should clarify matters and also bring out its main features.

The reconstruction of the record of social development in the form of a hypothetical sequence of stages was a chief task of 'the comparative method' of the 'classical' anthropologists. A vast collection of customs and practices from different peoples and places was made. Its extreme form can be seen in Frazer's *Golden Bough*. A series of isolated examples was picked from different cultures comparing those near the same level of development. No consideration of time or place was thought necessary. Tylor's famous statement is worth quoting here: "Little respect need be had in such comparisons for date in history or for place on map. . . ." (1871:6).

The argument of stages of cultural development emerged from the study of primitive institutions which were, in turn, used as 'proofs' (actually as illustrations) of the stages. The data used were of heterogeneous origin and often of doubtful pedigree. They were torn out of their historical and local associations. They could be fitted into any ready-made pigeonholes or could be made to serve any dogma.

Illustrative comparison has also been used to undo what the 'classical' evolutionists stood for. The case of diffusionists is well-known. The viewpoint of the leading American ethnologists in the first decades of the present century was anti-unilinear evolution. It was not opposed, however, to evolution as such. Lowie popularized the American viewpoint in ethnology through his *Primitive Society* (Lowie 1920:131). With Boas he shared the conviction that the proper approach was to restrict comparisons to well-defined regions. In practice, however, he did something else.

Lowie was in favor of empirically based general concepts. He himself established new categories, extended those already in use, and reduced the primacy of some others, particularly those which had been given too much importance by the unilinear evolutionists. In his *Primitive Society* he was not trying to build a universal theory. He was opposed to 'theories' or socio-cultural evolutionary sequences based on biological evolutionary analogies. He was not altogether opposed to sequential schemes. In his opinion "only an intensive ethnographic study in each culture province can establish the actual sequence of stages" (1920:337). He was conceptualizing from an inductive (i.e., ethnographic) base. Though it was not his main interest, some useful generalizations can be sequeezed out of his discussion. In fine, Lowie needed examples to illustrate his point and this is what he used comparison for.

The problem of the status of women is a good example to demonstrate Lowie's comparative procedure. The unilinear evolutionists gave rise to the proposition that matrilineal descent ('matriarchate') meant that women did not merely rule the family but also the society. Lowie declares this a worthless theoretical problem. Nevertheless, he examines it. Ethnographic materials from Australia, Melanesia, and British Columbia are compared to show that no better status is permitted to a woman in matrilineal than that in patrilineal tribes. The Khasi, the Iroquois, and the Pueblo Indians are then chosen as the 'best' examples of matrilineal communities. On the basis of these cases an a fortiori conclusion is that a 'genuine matriarchate,' in which the women rule the family as well as the society, is to be found nowhere. This example clearly drives home in Lowie's opposition to a priori theorizing. He is also opposed to the establishment of categories which do not have an empirical base. It also shows that in his conceptualization he remained at the level of the data.

Illustrative comparison is not restricted to 'timeless' stages or categories of culture. Something more general may also be aimed at. Radcliffe-Brown and Lévi-Strauss did this. For this purpose one has to conceptualize at a higher level of abstraction than the data. Radcliffe-Brown wants to examine the problem of mother's brother's position. He delimits the area. It is South Africa. The solution, which he has already arrived at, is the following. The sentiment toward the mother is said to be extended to her brother according to the principle of equivalence of siblings. This is supported by comparing the three illustrations, one of them comes from outside South Africa.

Like others who compare illustratively, Lévi-Strauss's use of comparison is only perfunctory. He says that a comparison does not result in a generalization. It supports it (1963a:20). A 'comparative structural approach' is supposed to show the basic similarities between such diverse forms of social life as language, art, law, religion, etc. (1963a:95). The supposed underlying similarity cannot be in the contents of the forms of social life, to borrow his own phrase, like myth and totemism. But he does not deal with the specificities. He raises the problem to an abstract and formal level. In the study of myth this formalism can be seen in the structural technique of the analysis of myths.

He hopes to demonstrate that the so-called 'collective consciousness' is, at the universal level, an expression of certain individual modalities of the universal laws which constitute the unconscious activity of the mind in space and time (1963a:65). It is interesting to examine the procedure he used to find support for his idea through the study of totemism. An initial comparative look at the totemic and Western societies seemed to provide him with the opportunity to prove his conception of universal mentalistic duality. He was surprised that the totemic and the nontotemic societies had been conventionally considered quite different. He could not accomplish his task if he remained tied down to the concrete 'symptoms' of totemism. By an initial implicit comparison he moved away from the symptoms. Some examples of the totemic societies were then selected and compared illustratively. He found the necessary materials and the recurrent ideas about man-nature relationship, which supported his 'theory,' in the myths. The most basic idea was that of opposition. Another implicit comparison showed him that the thinking process of the totemic and the nontotemic peoples is the same. Lévi-Strauss thus found a kind of psychic unity of mankind in the principle of resolution of opposition.

To sum up: the goals pursued through the method of illustrative comparison are varied, e.g., inferential history, to validate concepts and categories, to formulate typologies, to support general statements, etc. Either preliminary conceptualizations or preconceived schemes of interpretation guide all such cases of comparison.

The act of actual comparison consists in selecting cases, unsystematically, to 'prove' one's point. The technique of comparison serves as a device to obtain empirical support for a formulation which has already been arrived at. A distinctive feature of all illustrative comparisons is a lack of systematic representation of a corpus of material. There is no conscious or unconscious effort here to cover all societies or cultures of a defined region (or a subregion) or the whole world, or a representative sample of either of them. The anthropologist using this method chooses his examples either through his acquaintance with them or because they ostensibly support his contention.

What is the degree of confirmation for the conclusions arrived at through this method of casual or illustrative comparison? It is hard to say because the results obtained remain only tentative formulations. Even though the anthropologist may claim to have given empirical support to his formulations, in fact, they are not arrived at through induction. To borrow a phrase from Carnap, they are not confirmed inductively. There is no deduction here either. In reality the procedure is based on a combination of speculation and imagination.

(SYSTEMATIC) COMPLETE-UNIVERSE COMPARISON BY DELIMITATION

In the contemporary anthropological literature this method is known through one of its versions. It is sometimes called 'controlled comparison' (Eggan 1954) or intensive regional comparison (Schapera 1953). In our view there is much more to the method of complete-universe comparison than these scholars suggest in their versions. Other studies with different purposes are also covered by the complete-universe comparison. In all of these there is a common logic in the coverage of the material and the technique of comparison.

By a complete-universe comparison we mean a total coverage within a defined and delimited universe of discourse. Most common is a geographic universe, although it is not the only one. Such a geographic (i.e., territorially contiguous) order is not the equivalent of an ecological niche which forms the basis of some so-called controlled comparisons. This method of complete-universe comparison is systematic. Unlike the illustrative comparison, in the complete-universe comparisons there is one empiric order in the coverage of the material. In this sense, and in this sense alone, it may be called the comparison of comparables.

There are two main varieties of complete-universe comparison by delimitation based on areal coverage: (1) regional or subregional; (2) global. In the former there is prominence of geographic ordering. In the latter, for obvious reasons, the emphasis is topical and conceptual rather than geographic.

Regional or Subregional

For the purposes of comparison a region may be a whole continent or a small geographical area. We are aware of the differences in the magnitude which may arise due to such a broad definition of a region. But for the methodological purposes this fact is not too important as long as a region or a subregion is covered completely. If the region is not covered completely it may have to be sampled. Then the method is not that of complete-universe delimited comparison with which we are concerned here.

Among the first persons to talk about comparisons within a region was Franz Boas. He was for establishing historical relations between the cultures of a region. In his view, comparison was a suitable tool for this purpose. He called this the 'historical method' and was cool towards generalizations. It is striking to note that those scholars who were at one time or another connected with Boas and made regional comparative studies (such as Wissler, Kroeber, Spier, etc.) were not interested in broad and universal generalizations. They compared traits or complexes of traits. This approach to a regional comparison has certain specificities. Traits can be used to find similarities and differences in the composition of tribes or subtribes and for defining culture areas, to focus attention on the center of distribution of a key item or to trace historical relations between various ceremonies among the tribes of a region. The act of actual comparison involves checking up the absence or presence of traits in the list prepared for this purpose. Distributional maps are also used. Such an approach seems mechanical and gives the impression that it ignores the point of integration of culture. It particularizes rather than generalizes.

The (California) Culture Element Survey conducted by Kroeber and his associates was a regional study of culture-traits. Kroeber wanted to provide sharply defined minimal cultural units which standard monographs did not have. He did not find the data in them properly comparable. The Survey was to supplement rather than supplant the monographic type study. The scope of the study was limited as only the presence and absence of the culture elements were noted. It was thoroughly planned to include numerous 'tribelets' (Kroeber's term) which would not have been covered if the usual monographic procedure was adopted. But even in such a meticulous study the difficulty of isolating traits (i.e., the sharply definable minimal units) becomes noticeable: Klimek used 430 traits, Gifford and Kroeber 1094 (Pomo), F. Essene 2174 (Round Valley tribes), O. C. Stewart 4662 (Ute and South Paiute), E. W. Voegelin 5263 (Northeast California tribes) and V. Ray 7633 (Plateau tribes).

Stanislaus Klimek uses his statistical knowledge to examine the degree of co-occurrence among the traits in blocks of cultures or groups of culture strata. He compares these blocks in his list with those found amongst the tribes he wants to study. He also 'reconstructs' the history of the California Indian culture. Klimek describes the purpose of his work in this way:

The aim of this work is to determine the structure of California Indian culture and to interpret it historically. . . . By applying the statistical method, it has been possible to classify the California ethnographical data and thus to establish groups of tribes which have similar inventories and groups of elements which have a similar distribution. The groups of tribes correspond to cultural provinces in California. The groups of elements represent cultural strata. . . . These strata will give us historical facts . . . (1939:3; 149).

Kroeber, on the other hand, considers statistical treatment of the data only of secondary interest. He used statistics to establish relations between tribes or ethnic groups. He was very skeptical of Klimek's 'historical reconstructions.' "A historical reconstruction is difficult because . . . there is nothing within the framework of California ethnology *per se* by which to judge relative historical sequence . . ." (Kroeber in Klimek 1939:4). In principle he was not opposed to the use of culture elements for historical reconstruction, but California was not fit for it. Kroeber felt that the Survey was meant to define the California culture areas more sharply and to analyze relations between habitat and culture in these culture areas. Klimek, on the other hand, wished to try a bolder inferential procedure that involved many intermediate assumptions. Kroeber could not accept.

Why did the Culture Element approach not catch the eye of the fellow anthropologists? Kroeber himself points out some reasons for this professional neglect. They are worth noting. The following seems most important: Kroeber chose the cultural items and, apparently, did not lay enough emphasis on their integration. This was especially desired of him because his approach used and interpreted culture-historical data. However systematic his approach might have been — and it certainly was systematic — it was concerned with distributional studies which were not held in high esteem in the thirties. It is regrettable that Kroeber's approach was neglected. His method provides an excellent way to compare properly defined unit entities. It seemed particularly appropriate to explore the extent of cultural integration in a well-designated region.

One of the earliest attempts toward a regional comparison outside of evolutionary or 'historical' interests was Malinowski's *The Family Among the Australian Aborigines* (1913; reissued 1963). But Radcliffe-Brown's name is more often associated with regional comparisons than Malinowski's. Schapera and Eggan are two other anthropologists who should be mentioned here. The interesting thing about all these people is their 'functionalist' orientation. It seems this had something to do with their choice of institutions, groups or aspects of social relations, rather than traits, as the units of comparison. While comparing, the interrelation of the data is kept in view. The universe of discourse is clearly defined and delimited. Some kind of a general formulation as conclusion is always strived for. The act of actual comparison may take one of several shapes. It may consist of a comparative description of one or more aspects of all the cultures in the region and the general conclusion being the sum of all the common features (Malinowski). In another case it may start with the assumption that there is a single general type for the whole region (Radcliffe-Brown). One or two chief examples of this general type are described first. Classification becomes the base of comparison in this latter case. All the units are put in one category or another according to the degree of their similarity to, or difference from, the general type(s). A third approach (Eggan's) is similar to the second. In this case also a general type may have two or more varieties. Each forms a 'cultural division' more or less independent of the other. One of them is then chosen for intensive comparative study. A neat and uniform format used to describe the relevant material makes comparison easy and systematic. The general conclusions of such a comparative study may be further compared with the assumptions about another cultural division.

Are volumes of essays, covering a region and dealing with similar topics, examples of intensive systematic comparison? Schapera (1953: 355) has hailed Fortes and Evans-Pritchard's (edited) *African Political Systems* as a model of regional comparison and he is very critical of Radcliffe-Brown and Forde's (edited) *African Systems of Kinship and Marriage*. A third book which falls into this category is Eggan's (edited) *Social Anthropology of North American Tribes*. This last book was described by Redfield as a collection of essays on a single subject in which all contributors employed "a broadly comparative method" (in Eggan 1937:xiv). Fortes and Evans-Pritchard described their book as a convenient reference book for anthropologists and a contribution to the discipline of comparative politics.

All three books show a certain type of unity in theoretical background and subject-matter. There are a few essays which compare, but they are exceptions. The contributors to these volumes have provided materials for a comparative study so that, to borrow a phrase from Radcliffe-Brown, "a further step in abstraction can be made." Radcliffe-Brown has himself very aptly remarked in the 'Preface' to Fortes and Evans-Pritchard's book that "the present volume *presents materials for* the comparison of certain African societies with reference to their political organization alone" (Fortes and Evans-Pritchard

1940:xii; emphasis supplied by us). We agree with Radcliffe-Brown. A collection of essays, such as *African Political Systems* contains material for comparison, but there is very little, if any, comparison in it.

Global

Complete-universe comparative studies on a global (i.e., world-wide) scale are few, if any. In this class of global comparisons one might wish to include all known human societies, past and present. But the task of comparing them all is obviously impossible. It has to be selectively done. In such anthropological studies, historical rather than the conventional anthropological data have been utilized. Study of civilizations in the realm of anthropology is uncommon. If an anthropologist studies a civilization his approach is likely to be different from the approach of other social scientists including that of historians.

In one case the scope of the study (Steward's) may be circumscribed and delimited in an attempt to find out the conditions which determine a set of phenomena of limited occurrence. Julian Steward includes the New World and the Old World civilizations in his comparative study of the development of early forms of agriculture. He covers the narrowed down universe of discourse completely by including all the possible units. The civilizations considered are: Northern Peru, Meso-America, Mesopotamia, Egypt, and China. They are chosen because they show some common features. They were the cradles of civilization; and had arid or semi-arid environments. Similar developmental sequences resulted from the exploitation of a pre-iron age technology (Steward 1955:185). The inclusion of the civilizations from both the hemispheres poses problems of terminology and era-markers. In the present case the latter have been based on the emergence of new levels of organization rather than on any technological innovation. They are: farm villages or Incipient Agriculture; the amalgamation of villages into small states or Formative, the State being attained at the end of the era; Regional Florescent States and Multi-state Empires based on conquest. The broad categories of technological and social features form the basis for comparing the irrigation civilizations.

Julian Steward has used archaeological or historical materials for his study because they are considered relevant to social-cultural anthropology. His interest is not in morphological or stylistic types. An endeavor has been made to draw sociological meanings from non-anthropological materials. It is surmised that few concrete aspects of culture will appear among all groups of mankind in a regular sequential order. Cultural development is conceived in terms of the emergence of successive levels of socio-cultural integration. According to this limited cultural patterns and causal interrelation thesis, certain basic types of culture may develop in similar ways under broadly similar conditions. All the examples are taken up and analyzed not for their specific details but for cross-cultural regularities. Julian Steward's interest lies in ascertaining the causes of cultural phenomena and in formulating "them as laws in a scientific, generalizing sense."

The historical materials are dealt with from an anthropological point of view in another variety of the complete-universe global comparative study. A most notable anthropological venture, and on the grandest scale, is Kroeber's *Configurations of Culture Growth*. Here the units chosen are the great civilizations of the ancient and the medieval times from both the Orient and the Occident. As far as possible this defined and delimited universe is completely covered.

In this rigorous anthropological study the Greek and the Latin cultures and others representing the Occident are dealt with. Egyptian, Indian, Chinese, Japanese, Mesopotamian, native American and Arab-Islamic cultures are the non-Occidental ones which are mentioned most frequently. Kroeber chose such well-known categories for his 'inductive comparisons' as, philosophy, science, philology, sculpture, painting, drama, literature, and music. He considered only datable facts and gave a cultural orientation to all of them. He does not deny the legitimate role of a genius. He expresses only more fully than others the culture patterns and their values in the study of such a magnitude. Kroeber was fully aware that the specific characteristics of each civilization are not really comparable. He says that "the supposedly comparative activities are not strictly comparable. I concede the point; but know of no other procedure" (1944:21).

Kroeber's study is directed toward finding out some regular pattern, if any, in the development of the civilizational categories without destroying the integrity of the data. For Kroeber it is important that "the phenomena are preserved intact as phenomena" (1952:63). This fact and the lack of emphasis on generalization do not result in any diachronic laws. However, some awareness of the configuration of growth of the great civilizations and aspects thereof is brought home by his intensive comparisons.

To sum up: the two facets of this method which go hand-in-hand are the delimitation of a universe of discourse and its total coverage. The technique of delimitation works in two ways. In one case it earmarks a geographic area. All the units in the area are covered in an intensive comparison. The topic of study is anthropological for which ethnographic materials are used. The result of such an inquiry may be a limited synchronic generalization with a regional empiric support. In the second variety the universe of discourse is global. It is not possible to cover all the ethnographic data. This problem is solved by getting data from outside anthropology — usually from history or archaeology. These nonanthropological data are treated in an anthropological way to serve anthropological purposes. The delimitation in this case is not geographic. It is in the conceptualization of the problem. According to it the total available units are not too many. So a complete coverage of the universe on global scale becomes a reality. The outcome of such a comparative study may be some sort of a diachronic regularity, which may sometimes be limited or even vague.

Whether the regularity obtained through a complete-universe delimited comparison is synchronic or diachronic, it is a generality not a probability. The empirical support for it may not be global in some cases, but such a formulation is based on the total coverage of all the available material in the relevant context. A generality does not need verification because there are no cases to enumerate. It does not mean that it cannot be amplified or modified so that it may be used as a guideline for similar studies in other regions.

A complete-universe comparison by delimitation is an inductive procedure. The comparisons made here are not perfunctory but systematic. The conceptualization of a problem in this type of comparative procedure does not necessarily include a total anticipation of the results of the inquiry. They are at least partly to be explored by the act of comparison. Since there is no problem of the representativeness of the units of comparison in this method, bias is ruled out on this account.

HOLOGEISTIC COMPARISON BY STATISTICAL SAMPLING

A third comparative method is called cross-cultural by some of its advocates. "The cross-cultural method utilizes data collected by anthropologists," writes Whiting, "concerning the culture of various peoples throughout the world to test hypotheses concerning human behaviour" (1954:523). Cross-cultural, as opposed to intracultural, means outside the realm of a single culture. So any comparison between two or more cultures is a cross-cultural comparison. A notable feature of the so-called cross-cultural comparisons is the desire and concerted effort on the part of the researcher to cover the whole world. Köbben (1952:131) has proposed that this method be called *hologeistic* (from the Greek *holos* = 'whole' and *ge* = 'earth') method. It seems an appropriate name. So we shall call this method hologeistic comparison by statistical sampling or hologeistic (sampled) comparative method.

Like the second, this third major comparative approach differs from the first because it is systematic rather than casual. This kind of comparison is undertaken to find out the validity of some postulate or to test a hypothesis. The final outcome is not necessarily presumed to be the same as the postulate. It must be decided by the data. So the selection of the material for comparison assumes more than casual importance. The universe is to be defined. With some exceptions it is not considered either possible or necessary to cover it in full. The selection is to be made in such a way that the total universe may be represented. This is more conveniently done if the data are quantifiable. In other words, there should be some sampling and some use of statistics.

In the complete-universe comparison the totality is fully covered. In a consciously statistical comparison the universe is represented by a fraction thereof. There are two tasks involved here which need not be conjoined. The first task is to earmark the universe clearly so that it may be counted and referred to. Since anthropological monographs stress the specificity of cultures, their comparability becomes a problem. Comparison may be tackled through a device such as the Human Relations Area Files (H.R.A.F.). The idea behind it is not new but the attempt on such a large scale is certainly recent. The Cross-Cultural Survey was the earlier, pre-World War II, name of what later became the much expanded H.R.A.F. The second task is to apply statistics to social data. This also was attempted previously. The novelty of the Cross-Cultural Survey is in combining preparation of a worldwide catalogue of tribes and cultures with the application of statistical techniques on the samples obtained therefrom.

The 'statistical method' may seem to be the backbone of this approach. It is no doubt important but is only one way of tackling the problem at hand. In fact it is a technique which can be used to serve several ends. Tylor, who held that the future of anthropology lay in statistical investigation, wanted to establish that the 'adhesions' or correlations were not due to a chance association. Hobhouse, Wheeler, and Ginsberg (1915) were mild in their claims for statistical techniques and were critical of their own procedure. But they were convinced that the difficulties in the application of statistical technique to the social world could be surmounted. Material culture was found the most easily isolable criterion for measuring development in terms of the control over the forces of nature. It was also to be ascertained if any advance in human knowledge about the material culture is in any way related to the movement of morals, law, religion, social organization, etc. (1915:30). Neither Tylor nor Hobhouse et al. compiled any permanent catalogue of various tribes or peoples which could be used by them or by others.

In his excellent essay, Ackerknecht assigns a very high place to Murdock's *Social Structure*. In his view it brought about a renaissance in 'the comparative method' in anthropology (1954:117). Since the book is based on the Cross-Cultural Survey and is a fruit thereof we shall consider here the general features of the Survey rather than of *Social Structure*. Moreover, several excellent appraisals of the book are available elsewhere.

The Dutch anthropologist-sociologist Steinmetz expected to achieve the following goals through his proposed register or catalogue which he first conceived of in 1898: the quantitative studies based on the catalogue will prove the rashness of mere theorizing and will compel induction; the gaps in the ethnographical writings will be revealed and proclaimed and the results obtained will be irrefutable (cp. Köbben 1952).

There are certain common points in the Dutch and the American versions of the hologeistic approach. One or more elements of culture are considered over as large a geographical area as possible. The ideal is to have a representative sample of all the societies and cultures known to mankind. The attempt is to identify those characteristics which are detachable from the local conditions and historical connections. The use of statistical procedures is also included.

We should keep these facts in mind and should also remember that Murdock's statistics and sampling, although more sophisticated, are not different in the fundamentals from those of Tylor's. In such circumstances the talk of the renaissance of 'the comparative method' through *Social Structure* or even through the Cross-Cultural Survey is hard to accept. In fact, different comparative approaches have all along been used. Kroeber was right: "the comparative method(s) never went out it (they) only changed its (their) tactics" (1954:273). The studies by Lowie, Spier, Benedict, and Kroeber and his collaborators clearly show that the comparative approaches were never abandoned by the American anthropologists as was wrongly contended by a well-known American anthropologist. Eggan writes: "In the United States . . . the comparative method has long been in disrepute and was supplanted by what Boas called the 'historical method.' In England, on the other hand, the comparative method has had a more continuous utilization" (1954:747).

The ultimate purpose of the H.R.A.F. is to catalogue a sample representative of 10 percent of "all the cultures known to history, sociology and ethnography" (Murdock 1949:viii).

The other purpose is to test hypotheses and to prepare to formulate laws of human behavior. Murdock has more than once claimed that his approach, through the use of statistics, has reached the degree of exactness, found in the natural sciences. Two extracts from his *Social Structure* are worth noting:

. . . cultural forms in the field of social organization reveal a degree of regularity and of conformity to scientific law not significantly different to that found in the so-called natural sciences (1949:259).

Our findings suggest that a high degree of precision and predictability is possible in the social sciences and that allegations of indeterminacy, complaints about undue complexity and special pleading for intuitive methods are as unwarranted in anthropology, psychology and sociology as they are in physics, chemistry and biology (1949:283).

At a separate place Murdock further says that anthropology "if it rises to the occasion, may ultimately become the final arbiter of the universality of social science propositons" (1954:30; in Lewis 1955:268).

The difficulties associated with this type of study are many but two are especially to be noted. The first one is as old as the application of statistics in social-cultural anthropology. Galton demanded, in the course of his comment on Tylor's "On a Method of Investigating . . ." (1889), that the extent to which the institutions of tribes compared are independent must be made quite clear. This culture-historical objection is meaningful because of the statistical treatment of the data. Any historical connection between tribes will mean that for the purposes of statistical comparison they can only be treated as a unity.

A statistical treatment of the data makes quantification necessary. Only certain phenomena can be thus treated and they also are isolated from their socio-cultural contexts. This formal approach may sometimes result in mere enumeration. Another result of the statistical treatment is that the specificity of the phenomena is not recognized because they are taken to be identical.

Murdock had a sample of 250 societies for his *Social Structure*. His sampling is in no sense random. Is it representative? Of the 250 there are only 34 Eurasian societies to 70 from North America alone. Eight of the Eurasian societies belong to a closely related group of tribes in the Assam-Burma border. These eight units represent 250,000 peoples but only one unit is assigned to the Chinese who were 400 million in those days (Leach 1950:108). The sample is also lopsided regarding the representation of the peoples having different modes of subsistence. The unreliability of this type of sampling is evident on Murdock's own admission. When he dealt with 221 societies of his sample he found support for Kroeber's view on a certain problem. When the remaining 29 societies were also included the rival position taken by Lowie seemed more plausible. Murdock contends that in the matrilineal societies the term used for mother and mother's sisters is the same. The father's sister is called by a different term, i.e., there is bifurcate merging. Lowie ascribes this fact to exogamy. Kroeber thinks it is the result of unilinear descent per se (cp. Murdock 1946: 164-165).

In his hologeistic sampled comparisons Murdock remained in anthropological tradition with regard to the items of comparison. His use of statistics was also not altogether novel. At first he investigated kinship categories, e.g., patrilineal and matrilineal, derived from evolutionary anthropology. In his *Social Structure* he 'tested' hypotheses relating kinship terminology to descent, forms of marriage, etc. He was thus 'testing' social behavior 'theories.'

Whiting and others also test behavioral science theory. But they are interested in psychological behavior. Campbell, a psychologist, regrets (1961:346) that until recently anthropologists had somewhat neglected such studies. He also tells us why it happened: "Such research can never be central among the anthropologist's tasks, but can be invaluable in the consolidation of psychological theory" (1961:348). Some critics say what Whiting and others are doing is not anthropology. This objection does not seem valid. After all they are trained professional anthropologists and use conventional anthropological materials for their studies. So we shall confine our discussion to the procedure and the conceptualization which seems to underlie the approach of Whiting and his collaborators.

Campbell, in his defense of Whiting et al., distinguishes 'descriptive-humanistic' approach of anthropology from the so-called 'abstractive, hypothesis-testing' approach of psychology, which according to him has been also adopted by Whiting. He is quick to point out, however, that there are many things in common between these two approaches. We all know that most contemporary anthropological studies are as much analytical as they are descriptive. Abstraction is always relative to the context and the problem at hand. It is not limited to hypothesis-testing. The main issue is of isolability of the items to be compared. When Murdock dealt with kinship terminology he could, without too much difficulty, find the items in the source material he used. Whiting and others not only assume that the items and relations between them are present in the data but they rather impose their conceptions on them. Norbeck, Walker and Cohen point out (1962:28) that the Freudian source of Whiting's hypotheses has resulted in formulation of categories torn out of meaningful cultural context. Their quantitative scheme does not have room for the integration of the data. There may be subtle qualitative factors critically significant in determining the character of the behavior which they quantify to be measured. The actual act of comparison is found in assessing the scores on the list of disjointed items. It is not unlike the trait lists of the distributionists used to note the presence-absence data.

The common criticism against the hologeistic (sampled-statistical) comparison is that the data in their ethnographic samples may not be really fit to answer the type of questions asked. To this Goethals and Whiting reply that "no group has been more aware of the limitations of their data than those who have employed the (cross-cultural) method" (1957:444). They are quick to acknowledge the defect of their data but leave an important point unanswered: why do they not test their hypotheses with only more reliable and complete, though limited, data; or, why do they not test only those hypotheses for which world ethnographic samples are adequate?

Murdock's and Whiting's approach, particularly the latter's, makes several assumptions which are questionable. Whiting says that "the cross-cultural method, by studying cultural *norms,* holds individual variations constant" (1954:525). Whiting and Child earlier talked about "a typical member of the relevant category" (1953:25) but did not specify how that person was to be located in various ethnographies. It may be a practical necessity for those who use the sampled-statistical comparison but its defect is increased by assuming the homogeneity of primitive cultures.

In the comparisons between two 'ideal' or supposed factors, the problem is conceptualized with the underlying assumption that from one society to another there is approximately no difference between ideal and actual behavior patterns. Murdock accepts that it "is a very questionable assumption" (quoted in Lewis 1955:269). It is also not clear how studies of individual psychology will give us the necessary corrective which Whiting's assumption of cultural norms leaves out. Another questionable assumption is that a custom which is a basic unit of culture, is a special case of habit and so is fit for psychological treatment like the latter (Whiting 1954:526).

When two factors are related in such a way that whenever one occurs the other also occurs, the two may have a causal relationship. The former is called the antecedent and the latter consequent. Whiting does not use the terms antecedent and consequent for two such factors which occur in a single causal relation. By these terms he means to denote two separate 'causal' relations. For instance, in one of them a factor (child rearing) is antecedent in the causal sense. In another the same factor is the consequent. It may be possible that these two are properly established causal relations. But Whiting recommends combining two separate causal relations of child rearing "by virtue of the fact that they share the same scores on child rearing practices" (1961:355-56). He calls this the antecedent-consequent approach. It is an antithesis of the rigorous statistical verification of the individual hypotheses in which child rearing is either the cause or the effect.

It is difficult to absolve Whiting of the criticism which he and Goethals level against Mead, Hallowell, and other early students of culture and personality that they were anxious to fit a particular hypothesis into "some more general cultural framework" (1957:442). Whiting's plea that two separate 'causal' relations be combined into one seems to be motivated by a similar desire to widen the cultural base for his psychological correlations.

Whiting and his collaborators do not seem to be bothered by an important methodological difficulty. They take the natural sciences as their model of hypothesis-testing. So they use the logic of elimination to find cause. Since the days of J. S. Mill it is generally accepted that the 'methods of elimination' (e.g., agreement and difference) are not quite suitable for tackling social data.

By their explorations Whiting and his collaborators have shown that the extant ethnographic data on culture and personality are quite deficient for sampled-statistical comparisons. They have thus demonstrated what library research could do towards improvement of such elementary, but fundamental, aspects of a discipline like data-gathering. They have also embarked on a project to collect data more suitable for the type of comparative research they have been engaged in. *Six Cultures* (B. Whiting 1963) is the first product of such a planned and cooperative field research to facilitate comparison. Without going into the detailed methodological objections to such a venture, it may be pointed out that *Six Cultures* is not in itself a comparative study. Moreover, if Whiting were to base his comparative research on this book alone it would be anything but a hologeistic sampled comparative study which he considers the only proper comparative approach in social-cultural anthropology.

To sum up: hologeistic sampled comparison is a systematic procedure. According to some of those who practice it, it is the only scientific comparative method in anthropology. Taking physical sciences as their model they consider hypothesis-testing as the most important aspect of the scientific procedure.

The hypotheses are usually formulated properly as many of them are capable of deductive development. Freudian and Hullian psychology are the main sources of the hypotheses. Thus the problem posed may relate to individual or social psychology. The hypotheses are 'tested' against the ethnographic data which are obtained from some organized catalogue of world cultures, e.g., H.R.A.F.

Sampling, use of statistics and a desire to cover the whole globe are some of the other characteristics of the hologeistic sampled comparison. The emphasis on quantification results quite often in tearing the data out of their context. Its advocates hope that this procedure will result in general laws. Underlying this is the belief that "the data of culture and social life are susceptible to exact scientific treatment as are the facts of the physical and biological sciences" (Murdock 1949:30). Any conclusion obtained through the hologeistic sampled comparison is a probability. The actual result of such comparison is a classification or a correlation. Table 1 presents a tabular correlation of the four main aspects of a comparative method.

TABLE 1

A Correlation of Four Aspects of a Comparative Method

Method	Technique	Purposes (Goals)	Areal Coverage	Units & Categories
Illustrative Comparison (Casual)	Illustration	Inferential history; formulation of types, categories and general laws	Unsyste-matic	Traits, 'complexes,' institutions, etc.
Complete-Universe Comparison (Delimited)	Delimitation	Inferential history; limited synchronic generalization and diachronic regularity	Complete coverage of a de-fined uni-verse: sub-regional, regional or global	Traits, 'complexes,' institutions, communities and/or whole cultures
Hologeistic Comparison (Sampled-statistical)	Statistics & Sampling	Typology, hypo-thesis (correla-tion) and gen-eralization	Global rep-resentation through samples	Institutions

MISCELLANEOUS TECHNIQUES OF COMPARISON

The three methods of comparison, described above, are fundamental but do not exhaust all the ways in which comparison is made in anthropology. Below we discuss two other techniques of comparison not covered by the methods of comparison.

Comparison of Reconstructed Types
(Use of Polarities and Dichotomies)

There are certain comparative studies which are not about a single society or a region. The interest is not centered around a physical-geographical territory or even a socio-cultural unit. The ideas or categories, which transcend the boundaries of one society or culture, usually form the items of comparison. They may or may not have empirical referents. They are usually reconstructed after distinctive attributes or qualities. In extreme cases they may refer to ideal conditions which can only be approximated and may never be attained in full.

A polar type is an extreme case of reconstruction. At one end, the minimum, there is a combination of attributes which serves as the marginal or control case. The researcher tries to find a second case in which the combination of attributes is at the maximum. These two marginal cases serve as two points of reference. They may be treated as dichotomies or continua. In the former case comparison is supposed to reveal the nature of differences between the two extremities. It may also inquire as to what happens when the combination of the attributes representing the polar types is conspicuous by its absence.

Although E. R. Leach denounced comparison in his *Rethinking Anthropology* (1961b) saying, "Comparison is a matter of butter-fly collecting — of classification, of the arrangement of things according to the types and subtypes" (1961b:2), nevertheless in an earlier essay, "The Structural Implications of Matrilineal Cross-cousin Marriage" (1950), he compared the Kariera, the Trobriand, and the Kachin types of marriage. The three were respectively taken as the 'ideal types' of the 'symmetrical cross-cousin marriage,' the 'asymmetrical cross-cousin marriage (matrilineal)' and the 'asymmetrical cross-cousin marriage (patrilineal).' His *gumsa* and *gumlao* are two categories recognized in Jinghpaw speech which polarize opposite idea systems. We have not imposed anything on Leach's data. He himself talks of the ideal type and polarized nature of his categories as the following quotation from his new 'introductory note' to *Political Systems of The Highland Burma* indicates:

Considered as category structures the *gumsa* political order and the *gumlao* are alike *ideal types* which necessarily, at all times and in all places, correspond rather badly with the empirical facts on the ground. If this be so, it seems reasonable to inquire whether there is any analysable social process which can be attributed to the persistent discrepancy between the facts on the ground and the two polarized structures of ideal categories (1964:xiii).

Leach's account of the Kachin society includes the comparison of these two reconstructed types. He does not see any use of the term 'tribe' in his area (1964:xv). His study is not a comparison of cultures or parts of cultures. His categories are groupings of properties. They are not necessarily coterminous with the socio-cultural reality, although they may serve as a basis for interpreting the empirical reality by the Kachins themselves.

Comparison of reconstructed types involves something quite different when the continuum is in mind. One or more additional types could be placed between the two marginal cases. A continuum may thus be built to link the polar types. This is a good way to know the transition from one state to another. The act of comparison, in such a case, means not only finding out the limiting types but also the intermediary ones. In suitable conditions and with suitable data such a comparison of reconstructed types may be a most useful procedure for a study of generalized process.

In Yucatan, Redfield dealt with polarization of a different nature. The Spanish modern and the rustic Indian represent the two contrasts. The former is populous and the latter is sparsely populated hinterland. Redfield's comparative study includes two intermediate steps which form a sort of bridge between the two extremes. Unlike Leach's Highland Burma study Redfield's study deals with empirically referable rather than fictional organizations. The four communities dealt with are the city of Merida, the town of Dzitas, the peasant village of Chan Kom and the tribal village of Tusik. If comparable means similar, it is not a comparison of comparables. The units of comparison are, in one sense, intracultural. They represent different levels of organization. References to institutions are incidental. It is intended to see how the four communities, as organizational systems, fare in terms of several general social or cultural characters like disorganization, individualization, secularization, etc.

Leach posits his types as polarities. It is true that he mentions a stage between the two categories. It does not indicate an autonomous organization. It is not a step which shows a smooth continuity between the two main types. Redfield's reconstructed types in his Yucatan study are unlike Leach's in two respects. The identities of individual types are rooted into tangible social groupings or communities. Each stands for a certain degree of order and organization. There is a passage from one stage to the other because together they constitute a continuum. In short, Leach's types are polarities; Redfield's types represent stages along a continuum.

Unicultural Comparisons or Restudies

A restudy of a culture by the same scholar is usually a comparative study of change. The change may be in the direction of progress or in that of deterioration. In Redfield's restudy of Chan Kom the two conditions of the village — one in 1931 and the other in 1948 — have been compared. The material culture, the physical layout of the village including the streets, architecture, and the significance of dress for conduct and attitude have been compared. On these counts much more is unchanged than changed. Commerce, livestock industry, property rights — particularly individual rights — lack of commercialism, place of traditional and specialized handicrafts and production are also studied. The stability of social organization is examined in terms of the familial organization and the composition of households, the composition of population and the relation of the community with outsiders. The religious features and the changes in them, in two decades, have also been examined. The impact of schooling and the introduction of books have also received attention.

Raymond Firth's restudy of Tikopia is similar to that of Redfield's in at least one significant way. Both are accounts of how a traditional isolated, simple society reacts to the forces of modernization. But the nature of the original study determined in both cases the character of the restudy. Firth is more expressly comparative with regard to the states of the Tikopia society in 1929 and in 1952. The economic conditions and the influence of the external market is examined in relation to the standard and level of living, the nature of exchange — traditional and that with the foreigners — in light of the use of money. Rights over land, and their differentiation within the lineage, was looked into. Local groupings, patterns of residence, and marriage were also compared. In the broad category of descent groups sublineage, lineage, and clan were studied. The political system was scrutinized in terms of position of the chief in relation to the Church. The detailed emphasis upon the economic and social organization in Firth's study is quite apparent.

A restudy by a different scholar gives rise to some interesting questions. Oscar Lewis' restudy of Tepoztlan indicates that such a study does not specifically note the changes. The same topics are not examined in the two studies. Moreover, the previous study is usually not taken as the baseline which is so necessary to study change.

SUMMARY AND CONCLUSIONS

A comparative method has four aspects: technique(s), purposes (goals), areal coverage, and units of comparison. A correlation is found between the technique of comparison and the areal coverage of the material. On this basis we find three basic comparative methods in anthropology. Two other, relatively minor, techniques of comparison have also been discussed.

The first three comparative methods are most basic to contemporary anthropology. It does not mean that they were always basic or will forever remain so. One comparative method is by illustration (illustrative or casual comparison). The data are chosen and used casually for illustrations only. There is no systematic coverage of any geographical universe. In a second comparative method the universe of discourse is delimited and defined in some specified way. It is called the complete-universe comparison by delimitation. The delimited regional or global universe is covered completely. A third comparative method is distinctive because of 'representative' sampling and a conscious application of statistical techniques. It aspires to cover, some day, all human societies and cultures known to mankind. The contemporary advocates of this comparative method like to call it the cross-cultural survey (or method). It has been argued by us that it is better to call it a hologeistic sampled comparison.

The three methods do not exhaust the manner in which comparison is made in social-cultural anthropology. Two, relatively minor techniques are the comparison of reconstructed types and restudies. Unlike the three comparative methods the point of representation of several societies/cultures is not an important determining factor in these two techniques. The reconstructed-type comparison may be — in fact usually is — multicultural. The purpose of such a comparison need not necessarily be to build a classificatory scheme. Whichever goal is pursued, the bases of comparison are reconstructed types rather than cultures. A restudy is a very useful empirical procedure where rigors of a controlled laboratory experiment are not feasible. By this procedure, which Firth calls dual-synchronic, limited diachronic regularities can be formulated even for the nonliterate societies.

CHAPTER 5

A Critical Evaluation

Now we have reached the stage when we should look into some general and some specific questions in the light of our treatment of the subject-matter up to this moment. At first we propose to examine some objections to comparative methods in general. We shall then see the relation of comparison and control. After it we shall evaluate some leading comparative approaches to see if any one of them has an advantage over the others. What are the future prospects?

OBJECTIONS TO COMPARATIVE METHODS IN GENERAL

Extreme Relativism

Ethnographic monographs of single societies do not usually explicitly deal with comparisons, except in some temporal comparisons made in some restudies. Without monographic data, comparisons could never be made. An anthropologist's exclusive concern with a single people at a certain period of their existence may give rise to a viewpoint opposing all comparisons. In such a case it is contended that every culture is unique and possesses a set of values which is not easy to define. But an anthropologist, with his long and close association with the people, may experience and understand it. The uniqueness of each culture is inviolable. So there can be no comparison of cultures or parts of cultures.

There is some truth in this viewpoint. But the problem is not unique to anthropology. For example, animal species are quite distinct from each other. If their uniqueness was emphasized too much, they would not be compared and there would be no organic evolution theory.

Extreme or arch-relativism, if accepted and practiced generally, becomes an impediment in the development of any scientific discipline. In its reasonably restricted form cultural relativism is one of anthropology's notable contributions.

A corollary to extreme relativism is the objection to comparison in the name of functional integration. It may be argued that the parts of a culture are functionally related. Its implication is that to compare an aspect of culture with that of another means that both have been torn out of their respective cultural contexts. In some extreme cases this objection may hold good. But it can be overcome by a proper definition of the units and the items of comparison and by making clear also the level of abstraction at which one proposes to work. These points are often not presented in unambiguous terms. Radcliffe-Brown advocated and practiced comparison and at the same time believed in functional integration. But he never suggested a way out of this apparent dilemma. Malinowski (1944), who laid much emphasis on functional integration, was fully aware that in science isolability is as important as integration.

The French sociologists were critical of the nineteenth-century English anthropologists, Radcliffe-Brown tells us, because the latter did not realize that "two customs which seem to be similar may have different functions in the societies in which they exist, and are then not properly comparable" (Radcliffe-Brown 1958:162). As a criticism of the comparisons of the 'classical' anthropologists the argument is valid. If 'comparable' means similar then we can accept the argument, but not otherwise. Customs and social structures have functions. Comparison of similar customs which perform different functions and vice versa will reveal more explicitly the nature and form of both. Moreover, comparison of totalities, e.g., societies, cultures or communities, in terms of their internal arrangement and functional interrelation, to understand how a loosely structured whole is different from a tightly structured one, is very valuable and is badly needed.

One Well-chosen Case

A second objection to the comparative approach is put forward in the name of efficiency of one well-chosen case or one well-done experiment. Durkheim is the oft-quoted authority. He once said: "when a law has been proved by a well-performed experiment, this law is valid universally" (quoted in Lévi-Strauss 1963a:288). To mention Durkheim in this connection is confusing as he was also an acknowledged champion of the qualitative comparative method. As we

pointed out earlier, he thought that the method of concomitant variations was the only one method available to sociology. It is necessary
to quote from him here. He writes: "We must not believe that sociology
is substantially inferior to the other sciences merely because it can use
only *a single experimental method*" (1938:138 — emphasis supplied by
us). By this he means that the method of concomitant variations is
the only experimental method suitable for our discipline. The other
three (i.e., Methods of Agreement, of Difference and of Residues) are
ruled out. Durkheim says that "the so-called method of 'residues' . . .
is of no particular use in the study of social phenomena." Further,
"The use of the methods both of agreement and difference is difficult
for the same reason" (1938:129). No suggestion is made, at least here,
that a single crucial experiment is all that we need. This becomes quite
evident by the statement given below. It immediately follows the one
quoted above: "This inconvenience (of a single experimental method
for sociology) is, indeed, compensated by the wealth of variations at the
disposal of the sociologist" (1938:134). This statement of Durkheim's
clearly goes against the proponents of one-case thesis. There should be
no doubt where he stands after this unequivocal statement that since
the social phenomena "escape the control of the experimenter, *the
comparative method is the only one suited* to sociology" (Durkheim
1938:125 — emphasis supplied).

Among the contemporary anthropologists, Lévi-Strauss has voiced
opposition to 'the comparative method.' For him the only choice is
"to make a thorough study of one single case" (1963a:288). In this
he seems to have taken cue from the physiologist Kurt Goldstein from
whom Lévi-Strauss quotes extensively. A careful analysis of Goldstein's
statements in this connection only shows that he is in favor of a very
thorough study of each case. His procedure enforces "a limit upon
the number of cases investigated "(Goldstein 1939:26). The emphasis
on thoroughness is valid. But there is a difference between studying a
patient in conditions under the control of a physician from that of
the study of cultures. A physician can study a few selected cases very
thoroughly. An anthropologist cannot follow this example. So to say
that only one case should be studied is to go too far. There is an
obvious limitation in the study of a single case however well chosen the
case may be. Murdock and Whiting write in this connection: "We
believe that the day is past when we can depend upon an analysis of
single cases or single societies to give us scientific answers. We feel
that hypotheses suggested by the exploratory studies of individual
societies should be tested by quantitative methods in a large number of
societies" (quoted in Lewis 1955:267-68). We agree with the essence

of this statement. Nevertheless, as we shall show later the stress on the quantitative methods or even too many cases does not suit all comparative studies.

Comparison and Generalization

It is not to be denied that the mere accumulation of facts cannot produce basic concepts, generalizations and principles of a science (White 1946:84). The facts never speak for themselves. But in our view no types of comparison reduce down to the mere accumulation of information. There must be some efforts to draw conclusions from the comparisons. Failure to arrive at any well-formulated generalizations is not a failure of the comparative method used. It may be the result of several factors including the complexity of the material dealt with.

Comparison is no impediment to creative thinking. But neither does it substitute for it. Einstein is right. Inductive methods cannot by themselves lead to the basic concepts of physics or of any science (cp. White 1946:84). Rather, the validity of science rests on inductively testing and verifying the "free inventions of the human intellect." Einstein's remarkable theoretical formulations needed some sort of empiric verification. In our discipline it is not possible to do experiments. In Nadel's terms our methods can only be 'quasi-experimental.' Comparison is the only recourse left to us.

Leach in his *Rethinking Anthropology* opposes comparison as such (1961b:2). He says he is for generalization, instead. He fails to recognize the distinction, which is easy to find in a good textbook on logic, between generalization as a 'process' and as a product (Black 1952:281). A careful reader can unearth this distinction in Leach's own writing. When one talks of generalization as "a kind of mental operation" one means that it is, a way or a procedure through which one arrives at certain conclusions, i.e., a 'process.' While a generalization may be a 'process' and/or a product, a comparison is only a procedure or a 'process.' There may be several products of comparisons. Among them are typology, generalization, generalized process, etc. Leach makes a mistake when he considers typology-building, the only product of comparison. He does not like typologies so he lashes out against all comparison.

It is worthwhile to examine here the 'mental operation' or the 'process' that constitutes a generalization. To give an example from mathematics, as Leach does, is misleading because the principles of mathematics are not necessarily arrived at by induction nor are they always empirically verifiable. Peter Alexander distinguishes a general statement from a generalization (1963:105-106) which is pertinent here. A general statement may be a piece of mere guesswork. It may be right. But nothing is said about the way in which a general statement is arrived at. A generalization, as a product, on the other hand, is a proposition or a statement about a class of objects and is arrived at through an empirical-inductive procedure. It means that a particular case of A was found to be associated with B. This association was also found between A_1 and B_1, and A_2 and B_2, A_3 and B_3, etc. A comparison revealed that there was sufficient likeness between A_1, A_2, A_3 . . . A_n and B_1, B_2, B_3 . . . B_n that they might be considered variants of *A* and *B* respectively. Hence, the conclusion in the form of a generalization as a product is that every case of A is also a case of B. As a 'process' a generalization becomes a connecting link between the particular experiences of isolated happenings and comparison has an important role in it. In short, this example shows us that the generalization as a product is usually an outcome of a 'process' of comparison and a 'process' of induction-generalization also includes comparison within it.

COMPARISON AND CONTROL

Since Eggan's name is almost exclusively associated with the term 'controlled comparison' we shall examine here only his views.

The first use of this term was made by him in 1937. There it was said that a controlled comparative approach threw light on the historical and social aspects of the phenomena. In it one or the other aspect of a series is controlled. How it is to be done, is not made explicit. Our guess is that Eggan refers, in the present case, to the geographical-environmental conditions in the Western Plains. In his view they served as a controlling factor so that the social organization became amorphous and mobile (1937:93).

In *Social Organization of the Western Pueblos* (1950) one finds a more frequent use of the term. But it was his Presidential Address to the American Anthropological Association (1954) which made the term well known. Even there one does not find much clarification of the idea behind the so-called controlled comparison. In his pronouncements and in practice Eggan, like Schapera, is an exponent of regional comparisons. He believes that after a proper comparative study of a region is carried out its results should be compared with those of similar studies in other regions.

In an ordinary sense something is considered under control (or controlled) if it may be oriented in a desired direction. In other words, the factors involved should be 'artificially' manipulable for the attainment of the desired objectives (Ackoff 1953; Ackoff et al. 1962). Eggan, however, does not seem to have this in mind when he talks of 'controlled comparison.' It is viewed by him as a device to formulate not too abstract generalizations, the so-called middle-range theories. He is interested in controls or checks which will assure that the phenomena compared are comparable for scientific purposes (1950:9). This can be done in two ways. Firstly, only those phenomena should be compared which belong to the same class or type. Thus classification or typology becomes a prerequisite for comparison. Secondly, comparison should be made between the phenomena derived from the same historical source (Eggan 1950:9). This is legitimate but it limits the scope of comparison unduly. No statistical comparison of such a series of societies will be meaningful because Galton's objections cannot be overcome.

The use of historical and archaeological data, where available, does not make a comparison controlled. It widens its depth and makes it more rounded. The controlled situations, which Eggan talks about, are not devised by the researcher with a view to sharpen the focus of his research by manipulating different variables. They are, instead, such independent factors as ecology, contact and 'internal development' (Eggan 1954:757) over which the researcher has no control.

A better name for Eggan's approach is delimited regional comparison. He has himself once called it an 'integrated subcultural area' comparison. He quotes from Ackerknecht approvingly but misses a point made by the latter. Ackerknecht feels that 'the comparative method' serves as a sort of control in social-cultural anthropology where it is not ordinarily possible to have controlled experiment. Nadel expressed this point of view in his *Foundations of Social Anthropology* (1951) before Ackerknecht. Unlike Eggan, Nadel does not talk about controlled comparison. He emphasizes the point that, short of experimentation, there is some control present in all the comparative methods (approaches). Lewis also says that "the comparative method is the nearest approach we have in cultural anthropology to the experiment" (1953: 463), implying by this that comparative approach means control.

THE COMPLETE-UNIVERSE COMPARISON AND CONTEMPORARY ANTHROPOLOGY

In the last three chapters we described the different units, goals and procedures of comparison. In the preceding section of this chapter we examined some objections to comparison in general. Now we are ready for a critical evaluation of some specific aspects of the comparative approaches in anthropology and to discover if any one of them has an edge over others.

We have seen that it is not correct to consider comparative approaches or methods as coterminous with techniques. Case studies may be done for purposes of illustrative comparison as well as for the regional variety. In this procedure statistics can be used for inferential history, for demarcating culture areas or for global correlations, or for hypothesis-testing. Similarly, a scholar may use more than one comparative approach. Kroeber is an outstanding example.

It must be granted, though, that every scholar has the right to pursue the kind of inquiry he considers most valuable and fruitful. This freedom of choice is subject only to an indirect limitation. The overall intellectual climate of a discipline, which is a function (in the mathematical sense) of the stage of its development, is the factor responsible for some control. The degree of theoretical sophistication along with the nature, availability and the reliability of the data determine the type of questions asked. For example, at present it is not easy to seek diachronic regularity on the basis of existing ethnographic material. In other words, at a particular phase in a science some methods (or approaches) are more appropriate for tackling the problems than the others. Any attempt to sort such a suitable method out may involve value judgment. We do not pretend that we are ourselves free from value judgment.

Presuppositions and assumptions serve useful purposes in science. Any assumption can become an accepted scientific principle after it is established properly through independent evidence. An illustrative comparison in social-cultural anthropology is unsystematic. There is no proper regional or other representation of the ethnographic material. The examples are chosen to strengthen certain convictions of the researcher. They are determined by his need and his personal familiarity. The results obtained may be at times refreshing. But they lack the independent empirical base which makes inductive inquiry useful. We do not think illustrative comparisons are useless. Creative scholars have intuitive insights that they may present at first by unsystematic illustrations. Unsystematic illustrations do not constitute rigorous scientific 'proof.' Such 'proof' comes only from systematic, empirically-based comparisons. In fine, the results of illustrative comparison remain highly tentative.

In all intercultural comparison three things are important and should be made clear at the outset in every inquiry. The first is the *universe of comparison,* i.e., the spatio-temporal limits to which the study is to be confined. Secondly, the extent to which the universe will be covered in the study should likewise be made clear. Thirdly, the unit and the item(s) of comparison should be distinctly defined. The unit of comparison is the totality which serves as the basic isolate within the universe. It may be a 'tribe,' a culture or a civilization. The item of comparison is the category, part or aspect of the unit which is actually used in comparison, e.g., kinship terminology, cross-cousin marriage, unilineal descent groups, etc. The principles on which the unit and the item(s) of comparison were isolated should also be clearly established and spelled out. When all these points are kept in view the methodological problems of note arise in the hologeistic or sampled-statistical comparative studies because they aim to cover a 'global' universe.

We have seen already that the ethnographic monographs currently available were not written for comparative purposes. We do not mean to suggest that monographs should be stereotyped à la Wissler's (1923) "The Universal Pattern." Until recently, most monographs did not contain any quantitative data. If a statistical comparison is desired the difference between the qualitative data should be reduced to a minimum. It is not easy to do so. Thus in most cases the only variables a researcher is left with are the presence and absence categories. In terms of the statistician's criteria these categories remain only qualitative variables (cp. Driver 1961:304).

Sampling poses a real problem when a global representation is desired, e.g., in the hologeistic or sampled-statistical comparison. The first difficulty is that the number of all the units is not known. A large sample has a better chance of representing a given universe. Random samples may be considered superior by some. It is not easy to obtain a random sample in most ethnographic comparisons. It does not matter which sampling procedure is adopted; it should be representative. The difficulties of sampling are revealed nowhere more clearly than in the comparative works based on them.

For his *Social Structure* Murdock could not obtain all his data from the well-organized Cross-Cultural Files. In fact, only 89 of 250 societies were represented there. The rest of the material was obtained through traditional library research. This shows how the original sample of 89 societies was expanded (actually contaminated) by adding nonsampled units into the universe. Any claim of sampled representation, in such a case, becomes unacceptable. Similarly Whiting and Child (1953) did not rely on sampling alone in their study. Moreover, out of the seventy-five units only twelve were extensively used to arrive at important conclusions.

The Human Relations Area Files have come to fill a gap in our data-organizing devices and techniques. But the assumptions underlying the Files are not beyond cavil. The Files contain a sample selected to represent 31 variants of four major subjects. They are: geographical environment; basic subsistence economy; descent; and political organization. Language family is also taken into consideration as an indicator of common history. As Driver points out (1961:325) the mistake lies here in an underlying assumption that all the other aspects of a culture will correlate either positively or negatively with one or the other of the thirty-one items in the list. It is true that Murdock's 'world ethnographic sample' is an improvement upon all previous attempts made in this direction.

Keeping in view these difficulties of sampling as also the fact that the so-called quantitative variables of the statistical approach in anthropology are not really quantitative, should one recommend that the statistical approach be altogether abandoned? The answer to this question is no. The work of Kroeber and his associates of the California school shows that the problems of sampling and statistics are not only manageable but can be of service if a limited area is chosen or if the time span is short; that is, if the topic is not big or vague. In short, statistics can be valuable if the goals selected are modest. The weakness of statistics in anthropology is that there is no recognition of the specificity of the phenomena dealt with since all items are treated as if they were identical. A positive use of it may be made if this assumed similarity is used to detect certain regularities. These can be later treated separately by a thorough functional analysis. Murdock fails to do this, although he is not unaware of the possibility. Murdock says: "A special investigation of the factors predisposing a society towards one or another type of family structure would doubtless yield illuminating results. Unfortunately the present study can shed little light directly upon this subject . . ." (1949:36).

At the present level of theoretical development in social-cultural anthropology and the type of ethnographic materials we possess, the complete-universe comparison seems to be the most effective and fruitful approach. We want to say this in no uncertain terms that it is *not* the only valid comparative method. There is no justification for considering one method as *the* comparative method. There are several of them. The nature of the unit and item(s) of comparison, the conceptualization of the problem and the degree of anticipation of the results all determine the choice of the appropriate comparative procedure.

There are certain distinct advantages in the complete-universe comparison. It may be a subregional, a regional or a global study, depending upon the interest one wants to pursue. The universe may be delimited in terms of geography or any other suitable criterion. The regularity sought may be synchronic or diachronic. Both similarities and differences can be taken care of. It is true that the compilation of apparently similar customs, as done by Frazer is only the first step in a discipline. It does not by itself lead towards search for uniformities or regularities. But Evans-Pritchard's denunciation of any attempt to look for similarities is a very limited view of our discipline. A comparative method which only exposes differences is not of much use. Even for typologies we need to know both differences and similarities. Cultures differ from each other; this is common knowledge.

Despite the claims of its advocates and practitioners to the contrary, the hologeistic or sampled-statistical comparison is suitable only for exploratory research. As Evans-Pritchard puts it, "the method of statistical correlation can only pose questions, it cannot give the answers to them" (1963:14). Further, such correlations are only probabilities. Statistical treatment of the phenomena, based on sampling can yield only probabilities. We do not underrate their significance. In some cases these are the only results of the inductive procedures of science. Where the phenomena are randomly distributed, measurable, and properly quantified the probabilities are as good as certainties. But cultural behavior is patterned and not randomly distributed, says Kluckhohn (1954:959). He expresses the professional consensus that "the anthropological point of view prefers concreteness of context to dismembered precision" (1954:966). So we need to formulate generalities. They are not self-contained elements, from the investigator's point, forming 'similarities.' They are regularities which may attempt to reveal the nature of patterning, among other things. By defining and covering the universe of comparison completely one is not working to obtain mathematical precision. But one may attempt to formulate a generality.

The range of the hologeistic or sampled-statistical comparison is very much limited both in the subject-matter and the goals of comparison. The hologeistic approach faces a problem which Galton raised while commenting on Tylor's 'adhesions' or correlations. Galton said that items of culture may co-occur because of transmission from a common source. In samples, it is likely that, a single character is counted several times because it is not differentiated from other characters which are really its mere duplicates. Galton's objection does not apply to the complete-universe comparisons. In it the items are not weighted according to how many units they represent. Thus the relatedness of the units does not pose any problem at all. Such a study compares those units which seem to be really 'comparable.'

Intracultural comparison is a kind of systematic comparison about which we do not know much at present. An ethnographer usually describes the central or normative tendency of the society he studies. He arrives at the norms of implicit comparison. In a 'simple' society the range of variations is somewhat limited. As we study more complex and diverse societies the modal and normative tendencies can be arrived at only by explicit comparisons of the different groups and institutions or other relevant aspects of a culture.

The deftness shown by anthropologists in analyzing ethnographic materials is a heartening sign. The degree of abstraction attained in these analyses indicates that we are getting ready for more formal studies above the level of the empiric data. In not too distant future we may see comparison of models (in the general scientific sense) built after anthropological description. In this context Malinowski's concept of 'institution' deserves a more careful consideration than it has hitherto been accorded. The comparison of reconstructed types holds great promise for the anthropologist's study and formulation of diachronic generalized process. But we should be wary of too much formalism as in economics. It has vexed some economists and is likely to affect anthropology adversely.

CHAPTER 6

Ethnographic Procedure, Comparative Methods, and Explanation

INTRODUCTORY NOTE

One cannot afford to ignore Carl Hempel's work if explanation is the topic of discussion. Beginning with his "The Function of General Laws in History," published in 1942, he has expounded his thesis of "explanation through general laws" in a number of articles. Historical explanation, he claimed, "aims at showing that the event in question was not 'a matter of chance,' but was . . . rational scientific anticipation which rests on the assumption of general laws" (in Gardiner 1959:348-49). In a recent article Hempel has labored hard to demonstrate that there is nomological explanation in history also. He considers the genetic explanation and explanation by motivating reasons as examples of nomological explanation in history. To an anthropologist like me Hempel seems to stretch his point too much when he says that "the nature of understanding, in the sense in which explanation is meant to give us an understanding of empirical phenomena, is basically the same in all areas of scientific inquiry; and that the deductive and the probabilistic model of nomological explanation . . . accord well also with the character of explanations that deal with the influence of rational deliberational of conscious and subconscious motives, and of ideas and ideals on the shaping of historical events" (1964:31-32). This opinion is an article of faith with Hempel and other philosophers not on logical grounds but to 'prove' 'the methodological unity of empirical science.' As is well known, this movement was started in the thirties by Otto Neurath, Rudolf Carnap, and other philosophers of the famous 'Vienna Circle.' As will become clear later, the logic of anthropological explanation cannot be "incapsulated within any one single formula" (Goh 1970:340).

Some fellow anthropologists may sincerely feel that our procedures are not rigorous enough. They would prefer to use the word scientific instead of rigorous. It is common to contrast the procedure of science with that of history. But in answer to the question of whether history is science, Feigl says that "in as much as history aims at a reliable reconstruction of past events by a scrupulous scrutiny of present evidence, it is a scientific enterprise" (1964:477). It is notable that historical procedure has been called scientific even though the historian cannot observe his phenomena or experiment with them, does not quantify the data, and does not ostensibly seek to generalize the knowledge he acquires.

Writing in 1936 (reprinted Kroeber 1952) Kroeber expressed the opinion that experiment was not a fundamental characteristic of science. "The essential qualities of the genuine scientific approach are: first, that it seeks understanding as an end in itself; second, that in seeking this understanding it insists on starting from and with phenomena; and, third, that as it achieves success it destroys the phenomena by transmitting them into abstract concepts — laws, constants, mathematical relations, and the like. Hence the saying that science converts qualities into quantities" (Kroeber 1952:69). History and anthropology both share the first two attributes of science with physics. Like historians, anthropologists also preserve the phenomena as phenomena. Hence Kroeber's plea that the distinctive approach of genuine history and of good anthropology may be called 'descriptive integration.'

HUMANISTIC TRADITION AND ANTHROPOLOGY

From what has been said above it might seem that Evans-Pritchard was right in considering anthropology as one of the humanities. In the International Symposium on Anthropology organized by the Wenner-Gren Foundation (cp. Tax et al. 1953) Kroeber and Lévi-Strauss both stressed that the humanities dealt with their material at a deep level in contradistinction to the social sciences. But in procedural matters anthropology does not emulate the humanities completely, and it has important differences with history, which Evans-Pritchard himself highlighted (Evans-Pritchard 1964:186 ff). The reason for this is embedded in the history of Western intellectual ideas and their bearing on the development of humanistic tradition.

In the past, by common agreement, what we now call man's culture and his values had been kept apart as the preserve of the humanities. As one who represented the antiquities, the humanist was accorded the privileged position and high status he claimed for himself in the wake of the Renaissance. He was not committed to a particular philosophy or creed. With his gaze fixed on the life of man, he assumed "the possibility of distinguishing with some sharpness between man and the rest of nature" (Woodhouse 1969:826). This came to be depicted sharply in German contrast between *Geisteswissenchaften* (study of soul, spirituality, and mind) and *Naturwissenchaften* (study of nature and its laws). *Geist* was separated from *Natur* and was considered to be independent of the laws of nature.

The humanists were empirical in their approach as they started from the given and operated evidentially (Kroeber 1963:358). But their main task was to rediscover aesthetically and to relive the classical antiquity, particularly the glories that were Greece and Rome. The Renaissance humanists were also interested in their own contemporary arts — the only thing worthy of their attention besides classical antiquity. This is not surprising because the Renaissance was replete with the magnificent contributions of its artists and architects. Thus classical antiquity and the contemporary arts became two sources for the humanists writing on "the dignity of man, on human excellence and human felicity and on learned men" (Thorndike 1969:125). This was in line with the meaning Cicero attached to the word *humanitas*. In general it meant to him qualities, feelings, and inclinations proper to mankind. From the very beginning it was not merely descriptive, but its function was normative (cp. Woodhouse 1969:826). In one special sense *humanitas* came to mean humane feelings, consideration, and good manners. By the middle of the nineteenth century *humanitas* had also come to mean intellectual cultivation and the process of education that produced it. Humanities, therefore, became a group of disciplines which included language and literature, other fine arts, some traditional divisions of philosophy and sometimes history.

These poets, philosophers, and men of letters presented in their powerful language the insights gained from their personal experience, about man, his nature, and destiny. From appreciating the excellence of antiquity and the contemporary arts they switched over to value judgments. These aesthetic (value) judgments had depth but they could not yield a coherent body of knowledge. The humanities simply did not have systematic conceptualization. Kroeber is of the opinion that, since the humanities claimed exemption from nature, they could not have an "adequate intellectual theory system." The latter had to conform to the reality of nature.

Anthropology has encroached upon what had been the traditional preserve of the humanities since the Renaissance. It aspires to deal with its subject-matter at the same depth as the humanities do. But anthropology does not subscribe to the humanistic tradition outlined above. Evans-Pritchard notwithstanding to the contrary, anthropology does not believe in the Geist/Nature or mind/matter or library/laboratory dichotomy. The aspect of value judgments and the normative tenor of the humanities are also unacceptable to anthropology and its tradition. This will be conceded even by Evans-Pritchard. Evaluative-normative humanists are ethnocentric in raising one particular set of values as absolute. In contradistinction to it, "the barring of ethnocentrism has been a basic canon of anthropology for three-quarters of a century" (Kroeber 1952:137). Kroeber is convinced that this is the first step toward a scientific — as distinct from a humanistic — *study of culture*. He predicts that the future of anthropology lies in "the extension of scientific method to the field of humanities . . . especially that part of our functioning that will transcend present activities" (1952:361). Let us examine the implications of this.

SCIENTIFIC METHOD IN SOCIAL STUDIES

In his book, *Anthropological Research,* Pertti J. Pelto (1970:35) says that "the logic involved in anthropology is in principle the same as in all other scholarship." We shall agree with him if by logic he meant the desire to seek knowledge. But he seems to include more than this. By logic he means the rules of procedure which, according to him, are the same for anthropology and the other social sciences. Says Pelto (1970:xii), "most of the principles of research methodology that I incorporate into this book have been around in the social sciences for a long time, and they have been successfully utilized by a number of anthropologists." I am going to argue very shortly that this is not the case.

Pelto argues that in general the anthropological procedure is scientific. But he would like to see anthropological descriptions be more systematized and have more quantification and specification of research operations for use in any attempted replication. He no doubt states that "nothing in this discussion should be read to mean that all field research by single individuals is inferior. Far from it" (1970:270). But in the same book he has himself said that "the most pressing problems in improving anthropological research design lie in the structure of primary data-gathering — in the actual field-research operations" (1970:19-20). In fact so low is his estimate of this primary anthropological procedure that he is surprised, and somewhat disconcerted, to find scholars in other disciplines citing anthropological field data without serious reservations. The inherent contradiction in his position is both obvious and remarkable.

As pointed out earlier, Pelto is anxious to see that anthropology is assured of the scientific label. He seems to be with that group of social scientists who are taken in by the replacement of human sense organs in physical sciences by instruments. Viewed in this perspective scientific method is supposed to be a procedure which completely eradicates personal idiosyncrasies. There can be no disagreement with it in principle. But it is not correct to say that it is not possible to obliterate personal idiosyncrasies without the use of instruments. In terms of the overall empirical procedure and with regard to the aim of dispassionate and unbiased collection of data, anthropology is no less scientific than any other discipline. But it is a science with a difference and possesses notable methodological autonomy.

Many a philosopher of science holds the view that the theoretical social science ultimately aims at establishing general laws which should serve as the basis for 'systematic explanation and dependable prediction.' Some may feel that this aim was impossible to attain because controlled experiment, in the strict sense, is most difficult to perform. One might think that this settled the matter permanently as reliable general (empirical) laws were obtainable only by the employment of a procedure which had "the essential logical functions of experiment in inquiry" (Nagel 1961:452). Nagel thinks this logical requirement is met with by what he calls 'controlled investigation' which is different from controlled experiment. It "consists in a deliberate search for contrasting occasions in which the phenomenon is either uniformly manifested in some cases but not in others, and in the subsequent examination of certain factors discriminated in those occasions in order to ascertain whether variations in these factors are related to differences in the phenomena where these factors as well as the different manifestations of the phenomenon are selected for careful observation because they are assumed to be relevantly related" (Nagel 1961:452-453).

Nagel's so-called 'controlled investigation' is logically based on John Stuart Mill's well-known 'methods of experimental inquiry.' Mill was convinced that his 'methods' of elimination were suitable for the natural sciences but not for social studies — a fact which Nagel does not want to recognize. On the contrary, he holds that "the field for controlled empirical inquiry into social phenomena is in principle much larger. . . ." (1961:455).

According to Nagel, one type of experiment in the social sciences is called 'laboratory experiment.' As in the natural sciences "it consists of constructing an artificial situation that resembles 'real' situations in social life in certain respects, but conforms to requirements normally not satisfied by the latter in that some of the variables assumed to be relevant to the occurrence of a social phenomenon can be maintained in the laboratory situation while other relevant variables can be kept at least approximately constant" (1961:456). Anthropologists, by and large, will not consider this a very meaningful or desirable step to take in order to collect empirical data of anthropological interest. Nagel himself concedes that laboratory experiments alone cannot yield worthwhile generalizations concerning social phenomena.

Secondly, in a "field experiment . . . , instead of an artificially created miniature social system, some 'natural' though limited community is the experimental subject in which certain variables can be manipulated, so that one can ascertain by repeated trials whether or not given changes in those variables generate determinate differences in some social phenomena" (Nagel 1961:457). This type of activity is also not indulged in by the anthropologist in the normal course of his fieldwork. He is required to study the cultural setting and condition as given. Even when it is possible for him to do so, he does not tamper with the natural situation. Moreover, Nagel is aware that opportunities for instituting field experiments have been quite meager except "in connection with problems that are only a narrowly practical interest" (1961:457).

The third, and the most common, type of controlled empirical investigation in the social sciences is called 'natural experiment' by Nagel. It aims "in general to ascertain whether, and if so in what manner, some event, set of events, or complex of traits is causally related to the occurrence of certain social changes or characteristics in a given society," e.g., human migrations, variations in birth rate, adoption of new forms of communication, etc. (Nagel 1961:457). The anthropologist would not hesitate to take cognizance of such so-called 'natural experiment' situations, but not for establishing causal relations, and not as the main content of the subject-matter.

DISTINCTIVENESS OF THE
ETHNOGRAPHIC PROCEDURE

It is felt by some that anthropologists have now awakened to the necessity of a close examination of the processes of data collection in the field (cp. Pelto 1970:213). Pelto mentions Epistein's *The Craft of Social Anthropology* (1967) and six similar books to support his observation. But none of these books is a treatise telling others how to do things such as Lundberg's *Social Research,* Goode and Hatt's *Methods in Social Research* or Selltiz and others' *Research Methods in*

Social Relations, not to talk of Max Weber's *On the Methodology of Social Sciences,* Felix Kaufmann's book of the same name or Abraham Kaplan's *The Conduct of Inquiry.* There is a real paucity of contributions to anthropological methodology. We have always laid emphasis on knowing what it was we were studying. Unlike some other social sciences, say psychology, we anthropologists have not institutionalized our differences of procedure in terms of different subject matters — for example, the difference between clinical and experimental psychology. This has been possible because none amongst us has devoted his whole life in refining, developing ,and perfecting research techniques (cp. Lewis 1953:453-454).

Oscar Lewis talks of the eclecticism of anthropologists and their readiness to borrow whatever techniques are available and to jump in to do the field job (1953:454). But this field job (or fieldwork) has acquired a special anthropological color. Since the days of Malinowski fieldwork has come to mean "immersion" in a simple society. The anthropological fieldworker has to learn to speak the language and to think, see, feel, and sometimes act as a member of the native society and also to remain a professional anthropologist belonging to a different culture. He has to study a people and their culture in their natural ecological setting by staying in their midst for a long time. He observes the people in action and sometimes participates in their activities with a view "to understand the inside view of the native peoples and to achieve the holistic view of a social scientist" (Powdermaker 1968:418).

Anthropology is distinctive. It is committed to study *all* the cultures known to human history. It will be hazardous to predict its future course but its present priorities and emphases bear an unmistakable mark of its past history. Unlike all the other social or human sciences, anthropology has been primarily a study of 'other cultures.' Self-study is even now undertaken only sparingly. The diverse methodological implications of this fact have been scarcely pondered.

I hope many eyebrows will not be raised if I say that all through the history of their discipline, anthropologists have had a holistic point of view. The pioneer anthropological fieldworkers, at the turn of the century, believed in the total coverage of a tribal life. That is why in the monographs of those days one finds a description of almost all the universal categories of culture such as kinship, marriage, family, economics, social control, magic, politics, religion, etc. The anthropologists thought they could not be partial to any one category at the expense of others except at the cost of the holistic approach itself.

It is obvious that we do not mean this when we call our approach holistic today.

The contemporary anthropologist goes to the field with special interest in a particular topic. He prepares himself for the task by saturating himself with the available theoretical as well as ethnographic writings on that topic. Unlike the historian he learns about the concepts and principles which are of general use. The specific details of the culture reported in an ethnography are not what he concentrates upon. He learns how data on a topic are dealt with in relation to others. In this way he is prepared to treat his topic or problem holistically. He may not be able to go into all the details of economics if his primary focus of interest is kinship. But he cannot afford to ignore the role of economics in kinship. The anthropological fieldworker may not attain complete control of the totality, but its relevance is brought home to him in no uncertain terms. He acquires his data through person-to-person, or face-to-face, contact. Kroeber calls it holistic contact because this manner of acquiring data makes the investigator always aware of the larger whole, even if he is primarily interested in only a part of it. This is what we mean by holism in anthropology today.

Multilevel Investigation: The Particular and the General

The anthropologist does not look at the actions of Tom, Dick, and Harry as important in themselves. Harry is not known to him as a particular individual but as a person occupying a position. So his actions are viewed by the anthropologist not in the somatic context of Harry but in the extrasomatic context, to borrow Leslie White's terms. His oddities and idiosyncrasies are meaningful only to the extent that they add to or subtract something from the image the other members have of how Harry ought to conduct himself as a father, a chief, a shaman, a priest, or a warrior. From this it is clear that when the anthropologist comes to grapple with the situation, even at the microlevel, he must avoid getting lost either in the individual or in the psychological aspects of a person's behavior. He operates at a general level while he still remains with the data of a particular socio-cultural context. Thus he keeps both the general and the particular in mind at the same time.

The nature of ethnographic study, as of history, is in essence idiographic. But the distinctness of anthropology and history should not be lost sight of either. Unlike historians, we do not have spectacular events or personalities around whom our ethnographic studies could be woven. We also approach our data from a rather different angle than that of a historian. Moreover, the way in which we write up our material makes our ethnography quite different from historiography, Evans-Pritchard notwithstanding. In place of events we have sets of actions/relations, roles/statuses, and patterns/structures. Ultimately they pertain to the way in which individuals or groups of individuals live their lives. Though they are bound to a definite spatiotemporal context, they can also be viewed in a more general way. As Evans-Pritchard put it aptly "historians write history, as it were, forwards and we tend to write it backwards" (1962:186).

The historian's craft is almost completely connected with the scrutiny of available documents. The anthropologist, on the other hand, does not collect or interpret documents. In ethnography we create documents "by direct experience of living or by interview, question and record" (Kroeber 1963:132). It may not be inappropriate to contrast the duration of two years covered in an ethnographic field study with the long time span of the historian's study. The economist Kenneth Boulding distinguishes between two aspects of a system. According to him the "state description" of a system is "a description of the state of system as of a moment of time." When viewed from this angle an ethnographic account seems to be a "state description" of a socio-cultural system or a part-system in which the duration of field-work may be considered equivalent to Boulding's "a moment of time." If we want to understand what is going on around us in the field and wish to account for it, we have no option but to "freeze" time, so to speak.

Earlier we referred to the contention of Kroeber and Lévi-Strauss that, in general, anthropology operated at a deeper level than the social sciences. The microscopic approach of the ethnographic study adds depth to the basic cultural patterns which the anthropologist discovers and describes on the basis of his intensive empirical research. Not only does the anthropologist conduct his field investigation in a small territory, but the scope of inquiry is also scrupulously delimited. This is necessitated because he envisages his problems holistically. In one word, the anthropologist's approach is associative, not eliminative. The contemporary anthropologists in general firmly believe that these intensive field studies, aiming at tackling limited problems, are more useful for understanding the nature of human society and culture than aspiring for all-embracing generalizations covering the whole of mankind. We do not say that the latter are not at all worth pursuing. We all know, however, that at this stage of the development of our discipline we cannot attempt generalizations on a broader scale, with the same depth and authority, as we can do at the level of our micro-scopic and intensive fieldwork studies. We are in a peculiar predica-ment with regard to the community studies in complex societies. Our traditional fieldwork procedures seem to be apparently applicable here also. But a community study is a study of part-society and part-culture. It is not a holistic study in the same sense as is the study of an authentic, but isolated, island society in the Pacific. Ethnographic study is still quite useful. But face-to-face community studies by themselves cannot provide us with an understanding of the complex Indian or Chinese civilization because we are extending the famous "ethnographic method to fields where it may perhaps always remain subsidiary to dealing with documents already extant, but to which it might certainly make new contributions" (Kroeber 1963:136-137).

'Hypothetico-deductive Method' and
Its Relevance to Anthropology

In the previous paragraph we called the ethnographic approach associative rather than eliminative. This is a basic difference between anthropology and the behavioral sciences like sociology and social psychology. Within the delimited sphere the anthropologist operates freely and is not bound by a prepared research design. He has to per-ceive and to understand the totality first and then he has to make his own choice. The sociologist, on the other hand, may cover a much larger ground and may do so without referring to the totality even vaguely. He takes up only small-scale problems for study. The dimen-sions of the problem are carefully delimited in advance, i.e. the tech-niques are chosen with a view to test hypotheses. The inquiry is so tightly designed that only maximally controllable data are taken cogni-zance of. To the anthropologist this approach is too narrow and inadequate for analyzing problems where human beings are involved. We anthropologists are not willing "to draw limits on what we must take into account in order to understand a particular problem" (Tax et al. 1953:353). For example, if an anthropologist were doing research in a factory he would not confine his investigations to interviewing workers and the managerial staff in an office. He would observe people engaged in the production activities and would like to spend hours working himself, provided it were possible to do so. Unlike the confines of a narrow sociological or psychological analysis "any kind of anthropological research itself is a multilevel investigation" (Nader 1968:115).

Claire Selltiz and others have neatly summarized the steps of a research process for sociology and social psychology. They are as follows:

1. A statement of purpose is made in the form of formulating the *problem;*
2. A description of the *study design* is given;
3. The *methods of data collection* are specified;
4. The *results* are presented;
5. Frequently, there follows a section on conclusions and interpretation (Selltiz et al. 1962:9).

There is a clamor in these disciplines for hypothesis-testing. Some anthropologists also think that unless they test hypotheses they will be left behind in the scientific race.

A hypothesis may originate in several different ways. In order to become a part of scientific knowledge the consequences derived from a hypothesis must be verifiable from experience and found to be true. In other words, an effective hypothesis must be capable of deductive development. Unlike in Aristotelian logic, in modern science a hypothesis is an empirical statement which may come out as true or false when tested. This view of hypothesis is in consonance with the generally accepted "hypothetico-deductive method" of science. According to it a scientist arrives at a set of postulates covering the phenomena by "a combination of careful observation, shrewd guesses and scientific intuition" (Kaplan 1964:9). Kaplan also points out that the value of the reconstructions of hypothetico-deductive logic does not lie in their being mathematically precise and elegant but in the possibility of their illuminating the logic-in-use. This is what we want to know about the logic-in-use of the ethnographic procedure.

In his *Induction and Hypothesis* S. F. Barker has pointed to notable shortcomings which might result due to an uncritical use of the hypothetico-deductive method. Those who advocate hypothesis-testing in anthropology do so because they think completely in terms of advanced physical science. Little do they realize that even in the natural sciences the hypothetico-deductive method is not considered essential in all experimental situations. For instance, an experiment in medicine does not proceed with an initial hypothesis but according to the canons of Mill's 'Experimental Methods' (Ritchie 1960:175).

On noting the purpose and the background of hypothesis-testing in the natural sciences we find that an experiment may be performed to test a hypothesis which posits a relationship with this general form: "under such and such conditions, so and so will happen . . . provided nothing interferes." In assuming this the physicist circumscribes his point of view as well as the problem of his research. This is called a 'limited liability' or 'a closed circle of ideas' (Ritchie 1960:160). The physicist says he is going to examine a certain kind of thing in a certain way and thus excludes everything else and every other procedure as irrelevant 'to my purpose' (Ritchie 1960:160). We have tried to demonstrate that anthropological research cannot proceed with limiting the liability and by closing the circle around our data or procedures. We aspire to make a comprehensive and well-rounded study of man through our distinctive field studies.

I visualize three instances in which it is claimed that the 'hypothetico-deductive method' can be applied in anthropological research. In one case the anthropologist may be able to formulate certain relations which are of more general interest than the confines of his particular field study. He himself, or some other anthropologist, may take up this stipulated relationship and see if data from one or more other societies constitute a perfect fit or not. For instance, Gluckman postulated a pattern of relationship between bridewealth payments and the rate of divorce, and Leach tried to examine it with reference to his data on the Kachin and Lakher societies of Highland Burma. Evans-Pritchard mooted the idea of the divine kingship of the Shilluk and elaborated the concept of ritual of rebellion. Gluckman later tried this idea with the data from east African kingdoms. Śaraṇa (in press) has examined the Swazi case further and found that no ritual of rebellion was involved.

Another instance — a more systematic attempt to hypothesis-testing — is found in the works of Murdock, Whiting and the other votaries of the so-called "cross-culture" method (in our terminology hologeistic sampled comparative method). This application of the hypothetico-deductive method is not to a field or an experimental situation. Murdock and Whiting, etc. realize that ethnographic approach does not provide much scope for hypothesis-testing. This fact is clearly borne out by the studies in six cultures planned and conducted under the direction of the Whitings. The researchers here did not test hypotheses in the fieldwork. They collected data on a certain topic which could be meaningfully used for the so-called "cross-cultural" comparisons. Since to these anthropologists hypothesis-testing, or in Whiting's words jeopardizing a hypothesis, is an essential scientific activity, the ethnographic procedure becomes secondary to a particular type of comparative method in anthropology.

The third case points towards the possibility of hypothesis-testing during the course of fieldwork itself. Evans-Pritchard has pleaded that the conclusions of his study among the Azande should have been tested as hypotheses in the subsequent study of the Navaho witchcraft by

Clyde Kluckhohn. Such a study should be possible when the first anthropologist formulates the conclusions of his field study in such terms that each systematic study may be used "to test the conclusions reached up to that point and to advance hypotheses which permit verification" (Evans-Pritchard 1962:90). Usually anthropologists do not undertake the hypothesis-testing second studies of this type, unless one wants to call a restudy a hypothesis-testing study.

Some time ago, ethnographer had become a derogatory term in British social anthropology. A mere ethnographer was distinguished from a social anthropologist and descriptive ethnography from analytical ethnography. Evans-Pritchard (1962:93) was talking in this vein when he described Malinowski's *Argonauts of the Western Pacific* as "a classic of descriptive ethnography" to be distinguished probably from his own *Nuer,* a classic of analytical ethnography or social anthropology!

The assertions of the ethnoscientists that ethnography is a more useful activity than mere description is a welcome departure from the above viewpoint. The ethnoscience movement certainly aims at restoring the prestige of the fundamental task of doing ethnography. They hope to rehabilitate and revivify ethnography by raising its "standards or reliability, validity and exhaustiveness." Like other anthropologists the ethnoscientists also believe that the task of the ethnographer is not to predict but to state rules of culturally appropriate behavior. The model of an ethnographic statement is this: "if a person is in situation X, performance Y will be judged as appropriate by native actors," and not this: "if a person is confronted with stimulus X, he will do Y" (Frake 1964:133). Further implications of the ethnoscience movement will be discussed later.

According to the ethnoscientific approach it is not enough to account for socially meaningful behavior. The 'new ethnography' of the ethnoscientists aims at a "description of messages as manifestations of a code . . . [and] to build a theory of codes — a theory of culture" (Frake 1964:132). Frake and others think that to achieve this goal they have to test hypotheses at the ethnographic level in the field itself. On a closer look one finds that what the ethnoscientists actually mean is that by trial and error the anthropologist has not simply "to find answers to questions the ethnographer brings into the field, but also to find the questions that go with the responses he observes after his arrival" (Frake 1964:132). In fine, the ethnoscientific ideal is to avoid imposing any external categories on the native culture. This can be achieved not by adopting the short-term eliminative hypothesis-testing procedure of sociology or social psychology but by the intensive and long-term fieldwork procedure of anthropology based on *depth observation*.

Earlier in this chapter I referred to the methodological autonomy of anthropology. This point has been argued most convincingly in these words: "We are therefore thrown back for more on direct observation and analysis of the events and phenomena of nature (of which we should take for granted that culture is a part) than is the laboratory scientist. *To apply his procedures to our material is very largely to cheat ourselves. Our equivalents of the physicist's hypotheses are not something we formulate to begin with. They emerge gradually and pile up as we arrange and reinterpret our facts by trial and error:* they are mostly an end-product. Theorem, hypothesis, conclusion are not sharply differentiated but develop together. *There are strictly speaking no proofs in this method;* but there is an increasingly more concordant understanding of widening areas of knowledge and therefore a sounder understanding" (Kroeber 1952:3). We must never forget that anthropology is a field science and even today we have "no way to make an anthropologist except by sending him into the field; this contact with living material is our distinguishing mark" (Mead 1968:5).

EXPLANATION: THE PHILOSOPHICAL PERSPECTIVE

Explanation is a key word in the contemporary philosophy of science, especially in the United States of America. Some philosophers favor distinguishing something called explanation quite clearly from something which is not explanation according to them. Like the concepts of the physical sciences which are sharply defined, the term explanation has also come to acquire a well-defined meaning. It is not surprising as most examples, of what constitutes explanation, are taken almost exclusively from certain branches of physics.

In recent years Carl G. Hempel has emerged as the chief spokesman of this view of explanation. The following statement from Rudolf Carnap will indicate, however, that the idea has been generally accepted by many philosophers for a long time: An explanation of scientific charter "consists in deducing (a statement) from the law of the same form as physical laws, i.e. from a general formula for inferring singular statements of the kind specified" (quoted in Nadel 1951:191). There is an important difference between Hempel, on the one hand, and Carnap and some others, on the other. This will be pointed out later. Let us first note the Hempelian thesis on scientific explanation.

The success of Newtonian mechanics has served as a model for this view in which deduction-prediction is taken as the paradigm for all possible explanations. Hempel calls it the deductive-nomological view of explanation. The name, the covering-law model of explanation, given to it by William Dray has stuck to it. This explanation is basically "an answer to the question why a given event occurred or why a certain state of affairs obtains" (Hempel 1969:86). It presupposes general laws. Hempel is of the opinion that general laws play analogous roles in history, the social sciences and the natural sciences. Scientific explanation consists in explicitly stating the relevant general laws first. With the help of these laws and the particular antecedent circumstances, which are set forth as premises, the event in question, or explanandum, is deduced logically. Hempel and Oppenheim consider the following conditions necessary for an adequate explanation: (1) The explanandum must be logically deducible from the information contained in the explanans. (2) The explanans must contain general laws which are necessary for the derivation of the explanandum. (3) The explanans must be empirically testable. (4) The sentences constituting the explanans must be true. The whole thing can be schematically presented thus:

$$
\text{Logical deduction}
\left\{
\begin{array}{l}
\left.
\begin{array}{l}
C_1,\ C_2\ C_3\ \ldots\ C_K \quad \text{Statements of}\\
\qquad\qquad\qquad\qquad\text{antecedent conditions}\\[1em]
L_1,\ L_2,\ L_3\ \ldots\ L_r \quad \text{General laws}
\end{array}
\right\} \text{EXPLANANS}\\
\rule{8cm}{0.4pt}\\
E
\end{array}
\right.
$$

$$
\left.
\begin{array}{l}
\text{Description of the}\\
\text{empirical phenomena}\\
\text{to be explained,}\\
\text{predicted or}\\
\text{postdicted}
\end{array}
\right\}
\begin{array}{l}
\text{EXPLANANDUM}\\[1em]
\text{(Hempel 1965:249)}
\end{array}
$$

In order to be valid an explanation in science should be presented in the form of a logical argument. The argument should be deductively valid. Both the explanans and the explanandum should be true. The term covering law means that the event to be explained should be inferable from the general laws and the statements describing particular circumstances. Some philosophers, like Carnap, Ryle, Schlick and Toulmin, differ from Hemple. Unlike him they hold that scientific laws and theories are rules of inference rather than premises or scientific statements. The laws are to be cited in *justifying* an explanation not in *giving* it. According to these philosophers an explanation is like a proof by logical deduction where the rules of logic are referred to in justifying, rather than in stating, the successive steps of the proof.

Earlier in this section we referred to dependence upon examples from physics. In a seven-page popular account of scientific explanation all Hempel talks about are the law for the motion of the simple pendulum, Galileo's and Kepler's laws, Newton's theory of motion and of gravitation. The deductive explanation by covering laws can account for "the lengthening of a copper rod was caused by an increase in its temperature; or that a sudden deflection of a compass needle was caused by an electric current that was switched on in a nearby circuit, or that the Moon persists in its orbital motion about the earth because of the gravitational attraction that the earth and the Moon exert upon each other" (Hempel 1969:86).

If general laws play analogous roles in history, the social sciences, and the natural sciences we would expect Hempel to give examples of deductive-nomological explanation from the other fields of knowledge as well. Hempel contends that in history and in the social sciences the explanation given for the occurrence of an event may not be complete because an explicit statement of the underlying regularities is usually not included. Sometimes it is difficult to formulate them explicitly and sometimes they are taken for granted. According to Hempel such an 'explanatory analysis' of social and historical events is not an explanation; it is only an 'explanation sketch.' It consists of "a more or less vague indication of the laws and initial conditions considered as relevant and it needs 'filling out' in order to turn out into a full-fledged explanation" (Hempel 1959:351). In fine, explanation in the sense of subsuming particular events and circumstances under covering general laws is the same in all forms of knowledge — history, the social sciences, and the natural sciences (cp. Hempel 1969:90). As long as the historians and the social scientists fail to give accounts of the type, 'the lengthening of a copper rod was caused by an increase in its temperature; they are not explaining; they are only furnishing an 'explanation sketch.' Hempel and other philosophers are convinced that it is possible to overcome this shortcoming so that proper explanations in history and the social sciences may become a reality.

'All crows are black' is a statement of strictly universal form. It asserts that in all cases without exception when certain specified kinds of conditions (P) are realized certain kinds of things (Q) will happen without fail. In a statistical probability statement for the cases which meet certain specified conditions (P') there is this much (r) probability that they may have such and such further characteristics (Q'). Put in simpler terms, a strictly universal statement has this form:

"All cases of P are cases of Q"; a statistical probability statement has this form: "The probability for a case of P′ to be a case of Q′ is r." A schematic presentation of these two types of statements is this:

<table>
<tr><td>All P are Q</td><td>Almost all P′ are Q′</td></tr>
<tr><td>   x is   P</td><td>   x is   P′</td></tr>
<tr><td>—————————</td><td>—————————</td></tr>
<tr><td>   x is   Q</td><td>x is almost certain to be Q′</td></tr>
</table>

According to Hempel both deductive and probabilistic explanations rely on covering laws and "all scientific explanations of empirical phenomena are basically covering-law explanations of the deductive or of the probabilistic variety" (1969:90).

THE LOGIC OF ANTHROPOLOGICAL EXPLANATION AND CONCEPT FORMATION

In a recent article on explanation in anthropology S. T. Goh (1970:340) contends that "since as a matter of fact anthropologists are concerned with providing answers to quite different but equally legitimate types of questions, it follows, at least on a prima facie level, that the logic of anthropological explanations simply resists being encapsulated within any one single formula. Different orientations and foci of interests call for different types of explanation. . . ."

The traditional social structure of the Nayar has attracted attention of the anthropologists as a group of people who did not have the family as a social unit and in this sense they were considered an exception. In the last fifteen years it has been discussed in connection with the definition of marriage (cp. Dumont 1964, Gough 1965, Leach 1961b, Śaraṇa 1968). Here the case is being presented briefly for the type of questions the anthropologist asks, the answers he seeks and the source from which he seeks them. More details can be found in the papers referred to above.

Traditionally the residential group among the Nayars was a property group or a *tarvad*. All the members of the *tarvad* were consanguineal kin. The descent was matrilineal, the residence was matrilocal, designations were matronymic, and the *tarvad* property was passed on from mother to daughter. The female members were very important to the *tarvad*. They begot children for it and thus insured its continuance. The Nayars were warriors by profession. Most of the able-bodied men had to go out on military service for long stretches of time. Linked-lineages or *enangar* were socially very significant among the Nayars.

The girls were allowed to have liaison with more than one man. One of the reasons may have been the absence of the menfolk due to their military duties elsewhere. The society could not be too harsh on its most important members, namely, the young and fertile women. The private affair of sexual relations was left to the two partners. There was permissiveness but not promiscuity. The society put up two barriers of great social significance. Firstly, before she attained her puberty a girl had to go through *tali kettu kalyanam* (tali-tying 'marriage'). A boy from the appropriate linked-lineage tied a golden *tali* around the neck of a Nayar girl publicly and thus became her 'ritual husband.' After the couple had been in seclusion for three days the 'ritual husband's' departure was marked with the tearing in public of the loincloth worn by the girl during seclusion. The 'ritual husband' does not retain any special privileges with his ritual wife. She is not obliged to have him as her sexual partner. Thus rather than having any 'monopoly in his wife's sexuality' a ritual husband may not even have access to it. This is a rather unique case and the ethnographer has to explain it. The people know the rules of appropriate behavior and act according to the demand of particular situations. The anthropologist has to give his account on the basis of his understanding including both the acts of behavior and the rules which are supposed to be followed. This will have to be context-bound lest it should become meaningless. The general laws of marriage that will be cited my a philosopher-logician or a sociologist born and enculturated in the West will be culture-bound and will not be useful in accounting for the facts of the Nayar case.

Let us now take up the second social barrier which the traditional Nayar society used to erect for its womenfolk who were permitted considerable freedom in choosing their sexual partners after the *tali*-tying ceremony. It had to do with the pregnancy of the girl. The conceived child must be legitimized before he/she can acquire the right of membership of and the right to be raised in the mother's *tarvad*. This becomes most essential because of the very special kind of matrilineal system of the Nayar. The residence rules do not permit the husband to share the same roof with his wife in a matrlineal-uxorilocal pattern of residence. But in most such systems the male partner has complete or nearly complete monopoly in his wife's sexuality. This was not so among the Nayars. Therefore, the society felt the necessity to make sure that the pregnant woman had used her sexual freedom properly. It was essential that she pass this test because in the caste ideology hypergamy was permissible but hypogamous unions were out of the question.

A word about the Nambudiri-Nayar unions is necessary here. According to the patrilineal Nambudiri only the eldest brother in a family could have a proper marriage with a Nambudiri wife. The younger brothers were permitted to have *sambandham* relations with the Nayar women. The Nambudiris may hold that these were not marriages but only concubinages. This is wrong because concubinage has meaning in a patrilineal system where the concubine and the children born to her are accorded jural rights according to custom. But the Nambudiri 'visiting husbands' had no such obligations and the children born to their Nayar mates belonged to the mother's *tarvad*. From the Nayar point of view, if the Nambudiri male agrees to tie a *tali* round the neck of a royal or a high caste Nayar girl as a ritual husband and agrees to meet the delivery charges when his *sambandham* Nayar mate conceives, he has fulfilled his obligations and has helped in establishing the legitimacy of the sexual union and the result of that, i.e., the child to be born.

I think such an account, though it pertains to a specific case, is very sophisticated. I fail to understand why such an account cannot be called an explanation even though no general laws are involved and no deduction has been made. This cannot be called merely a description. It is a *contextual explanation*.

Michael Scriven is very critical of the covering law model of explanation. In 1959 he said that explanations are "practical, context-bound affairs" (Scriven 1959:450). In some cases Hempel's grandiose deductive-nomological "complete explanation" may be too little and in some cases it may be too much. For instance, we want to explain Nayar marriage. This particular phenomenon can be explained by isolating the conditions under which it occurs. This might seem to be quite simple to the philosopher but is acceptable to the anthropologist. The anthropologist might argue that in his account of the Nayar marriage he was isolating conditions under which this unique institution flourished. But the philosopher has something else in his mind. To him "a logical condition for this isolation was the existence of a generalization or generalizations" (Harré 1965:82).

What sort of generalizations might help? Human beings have a sexual urge which must be gratified. Uncontrolled or unregulated sexual gratification will not be conducive to the formation of social groups. The formation of viable social groups is a basic condition of human existence. Sex, then, must be regulated. The institution of marriage regulates sex. Since in all known human societies sex is regulated through marriage and the Nayars are a viable social group (society), sex, therefore, is regulated among them through the institution of marriage. These general statements are probably true but they fail to tell us why the traditional Nayars married in the way they are known to have married. One of the deficiencies in these general statements is that they take for granted that marriage is universal and can be defined that way. In fact, it is an empirical rather than a logical question. As we have seen above, it is not feasible to formulate general laws of marriage and then to deduce the Nayar form of marriage as an empirical proposition. Even if one could do so one would not be accounting for the Nayar marriage and, therefore, would not be explaining it. In Scriven's words, a scientific explanation is "a topically unifield communication, the content of which imparts understanding of some scientific phenomena" (1962.224-25). This meaning of the term 'explanation' makes sense. This is what good anthropologists do in their basic researches.

As we saw in the case of Nayar marriage some problems which the anthropologists tackle are of local nature. But they may have much wider implications. Let us take the other case mentioned by Evans-Pritchard in his *Kinship and Marriage Among the Nuer:*

> What seems to us, but not at all to Nuer, a somewhat strange union is that in which a woman marries another woman and counts as the pater of the children born to the wife. Such marriages are by no means uncommon in Nuerland, and they must be regarded as a form of simple legal marriage, for the woman-husband marries her wife in exactly the same way as a man marries a woman . . . the husband gets a male kinsman or friend or neighbour . . . to beget children by his wife. . . . We may perhaps refer to this kind of union as woman-marriage (1960:108).

> A very common feature of Nuer social life is a union I have called ghost-marriage. If a man dies without legal male heirs, a kinsman of his or the succeeding generation . . . ought to take a wife to his name . . . it is understood that it is not he, but the dead man, who is the legal husband (1960:109).

The basic question is what to do with these apparently 'outlandish' practices prevalent among the Nuer. Should we accept these as "a form of simple legal marriage" as Evans-Pritchard has suggested or consider them as a strange case of unisexual union which cannot be called a marriage? The anthropological answer to this question is unequivocal. Our basic premise is that the customs and the institutions of a people must be recorded and presented in their native color and form. In ethnographies no distortion can be allowed to creep in, either consciously or unconsciously. In these conditions it is logical that the

Nuer "marriages" be accounted for contextually because no general principles of marriage — even if they could be enunciated — would be of any help in improving our understanding of the said cases.

I must hasten to add that the story does not end here. Anthropology's interests are not exhausted by such contextual explanations of particular sets of phenomena. If we are interested in the Nuer marriage, the Nayar marriage, or the Greek marriage, we are no less interested in the general concept of marriage. There must be some way to find a rationale for the use of the term marriage for such diverse practices as the 'contractual-free-choice marriage' in the West, the 'sacramental-arranged marriage' among the Hindus and the Nuer 'woman-marriage' and 'ghost-marriage.' The difficulties are so immense that a leading anthropologist once remarked: "all universal definitions of marriage are vain" (Leach 1961b:105). Leach notwithstanding, we have to have some general concept of such an important and universal category of culture as marriage. What is involved in this case is not explanation but, what Hempel has called, concept formation. The only possible way to do it is through the application of a comparative method so that the specificity of a particular culture may be transcended.

Ethnography is vital to anthropology, but comparison is equally basic. The ultimate aim of anthropology is to understand the similarities and differences among human cultures and to throw light on what is glibly called 'human nature.' This cannot be attained through the contextual explanations. I am aware that I am not saying anything new because others have already stressed this point. I am providing only a methodological reason for calling anthropology a comparative discipline. Elsewhere I have said that

our anthropological method has two parts. Each part, though related, is independent of the other. Two different researchers may carry on the two parts separately. Observation and the recording of the data together constitute one phase of the anthropological method [called here the ethnographic procedure]. The other phase consists of comparison done in the library. This the anthropological method is quite different from the combined observation-and-experiment procedure of the natural sciences. The implication of this procedural difference should not be lost sight of in any discussion of anthropological methodology (Śaraṇa: in press).

Here I am pointing out that through the ethnographic procedure we arrive at contextual explanations and the comparative methods help us in concept formation and concept clarification.

Peter Winch (1958) is an advocate of the view that the only thing possible through a social inquiry is the particularity of concepts.

He cites Evans-Pritchard's works on the Azande as the model work by an anthropologist who knows his job. Alasdair MacIntyre (1967) seeks to prove by citing Leach's critique of Evans-Pritchard in his *Pul Eliya* and Walter Goldschmidt's *Comparative Functionalism* that these anthropologists think that Evans-Pritchard's is not the only way. Winch and MacIntyre both are only partly correct. As anthropologists we have to do both things which neither exclude each other nor are unconnected.

The so-called "conceptual particularism" is not a speciality of Evans-Pritchard's brand of anthropology alone. A great and early champion of it was Malinowski whom MacIntyre quotes with approval against Winch. Some people even accused Malinowski of looking at the whole world through Trobriand eyes. Evans-Pritchard himself once prescribed that every anthropologist should do fieldwork in at least two different and unrelated cultures. This was thought to be necessary to avoid obsession with the data and concepts from a simple field experience. All good ethnography is done today with this underlying professional belief that the anthropologist will be able to analyze and interpret his data properly only with reference to context. I shall call it "contextual-functional perspective" rather than conceptual particularism. In actuality, as has been already pointed out above, the concepts which the social-cultural anthropologist uses in his description and analysis of a particular society or its institutions have a general rather than a specific connotation. For instance, Evans-Pritchard's use of the word marriage for those 'strange' Nuer customs raised an important problem of definition of marriage which is outside the scope of 'conceptual particularism.'

Some American social-cultural anthropologists have thrown new light on conceptual particularism. Influenced by linguistics these anthropologists, so to speak, turned inward and discovered that ethnography was the most useful part of the anthropological work as it was based on fieldwork through the native tongue. They are in favor of making it more systematic and scientific. They call their approach 'ethnoscience.' They think that it is not enough to seek answers to questions in the culture the anthropologist is studying. It is necessary to find the questions themselves in the native culture. This is in complete accord with Malinowski's ground-breaking Trobriand study through which he began the revolutionary step of subjecting individual cultures to a detailed internal analysis. Frake presents the ethnoscientific perspective of 'the New Ethnography' in these words: "The image of an ethnography we have in mind also includes lists of queries and responses, but with this difference: both the queries and their responses are to be discovered in the culture of the people being studied. The problem is not simply to find answers to questions the ethnographer brings into the field, but also to find the questions that go with the responses he observes after his arrival" (1964:132). The goal set by the ethnoscientists is to get inside their subjects' heads.

We may sum up the discussion of this section thus: Goh is willing to concede that the kind of questions anthropologists ask have to be tackled in more than one way. In his view, "methodological eclecticism seems the only sensible attitude to adopt" (1970:340). Even in doing so he does not abandon the ideal of deductive-nomological explanation. He seems to entertain the possibility of a covering law model of explanation even in anthropology of tomorrow. It is difficult to say whether we will really have this type of explanation in the future. However, it does not seem to be even a remote possibility.

In contemporary anthropology we have neither a deductive-nomological nor a statistical explanation. This is no cause to lament. In Nicholas Rescher's words "notwithstanding its erstwhile stature, and despite occasional flurries of nostalgia for its comfortable simplicities, the deductive conception of explanation must yield up its claims to provide a comprehensive account of the nature of scientific explanation" (1963:58). Our ethnographic procedures provide us with contextual explanations.

Our comparative procedures do not give us explanations. They are the means for concept formation and concept clarification. This is no cause for anxiety. Rescher points out that even in the natural sciences today it is considered a mistake "to suppose the definitive task of science to be the explanation of the states of natural systems" (1963:55). The main task of science is believed to be "rationalization" or "systematization" through which one should be able to find out the laws that "govern the functioning of natural processes" (Rescher 1963:56). Let us hope we shall also proceed on our path of finding out what governs the functioning of socio-cultural processes and systems and comparative methods will contribute their own share in accomplishing this task.

References

Ackerknecht, Edwin H.
  1954   On the comparative method in anthropology. In *Method and per-*
          spective in anthropology, ed. Robert F. Spencer. Minneapolis: Uni-
          versity of Minnesota Press.
Ackoff, Russell L.
  1953   *The design of research.* Chicago: University of Chicago Press.
Ackoff, Russell L. et al.
  1962   *Scientific method: optimizing applied research decisions.* New York:
          John Wiley and Sons.
Alexander, Peter
  1963   *A preface to the logic of science.* London: Ward and Sheed.
Barker, S. F.
  1957   *Induction and hypothesis: a study of the logic of confirmation.* Ithaca,
          New York: Cornell University Press.
Becker, Howard
  1940   Historical sociology. In *Contemporary social theory,* eds. H. E. Barnes,
          H. Becker and F. B. Becker. New York: Appleton-Century Com-
          pany, Inc.
Becker, Howard and H. E. Barnes
  1952   *Social thought from lore to science.* 2nd ed. Washington, D.C.:
          Harren Press. (Originally published in 1938.)
Benedict, Ruth
  1934   *Patterns of culture.* Boston: Houghton Mifflin Company.
Black, Max
  1952   *Critical thinking: an introduction to logic and scientific method.* 2nd
          rev. ed. New York: Prentice-Hall, Inc.
Boas, Franz
  1896   The limitations of the comparative method. *Science,* N. S., 4:901-908.
          (Reprinted in Franz Boas. *Race, langauge and culture.* New York:
          The Macmillan Company.)
  1936   Invention. In *General anthropology,* ed. Franz Boas. New York:
          D. C. Heath and Co.
  1940   *Race, language and culture.* New York: The Macmillan Company.
Boulding, Kenneth
  1961   *Image: knowledge in life and society.* Ann Arbor: The University of
          Michigan Press.
Braithwaite, R. D.
  1962   Models in the empirical sciences. In *Logic, methodology and Philoso-*
          phy of science, eds. E. Nagel, P. Suppes and A. Tarski. Stanford:
          Stanford University Press.

Campbell, Donald T.
  1961   The mutual methodological relevance of anthropology and psychology. In *Psychological anthropology,* ed. Francis L. K. Hsu. Homewood, Illinois: The Dorsey Press, Inc.
Carnap, Rudolph
  1953   Inductive logic and science. *Proceedings of the American Academy of Arts and Sciences* (Boston) 80:189-197.
Cohen, Morris Raphael
  1964   *Reason and nature: the meaning of the scientific method.* New York: The Free Press of Glencoe.
Copi, Irving M. and James A. Gould (eds.)
  1964   *Readings in logic.* New York: The Macmillan Company.
Culin, S.
  1902   American Indian games. *American Anthropologist* 4:58-64.
  1907   Games of the North American Indians. 24th Annual Report, Bureau of American Ethnology, Washington D.C.
Driver, Harold A.
  1961   Introduction to statistic for comparative research. In *Readings in cross-cultural methodology,* ed. Frank W. Moore. New Haven, Conn.: HRAF Press.
Dumont, Louis
  1964   Marriage in India: the present state of the question. Postscript to Part I-II: Nayar and Newar. *Contributions to Indian Sociology* VII: 77-98.
Durkheim, Emile
  1938   *The rules of sociological method.* Chicago: The University of Chicago Press.
Eaton, R. M.
  1931   *General logic.* New York: Scribner.
Eggan, Fred
  1950   *Social organization of the Western Pueblos.* Chicago: The University of Chicago Press.
  1954   Social anthropology and the method of controlled comparison. *American Anthropologist* 56:743-763.
Eggan, Fred, ed.
  1955   *Social anthropology of North American tribes.* Chicago: The University of Chicago Press. (Originally published in 1937.)
Eisenstadt, S. N.
  1954   African age groups, a comparative study. *Africa* 24:100-113.
  1959   Primitive political systems: a preliminary comparative analysis. *American Anthropologist* 61:200-220.
Epistein, A. L., ed.
  1967   *The craft of social anthropology.* London: Social Science Paperbacks in association with Tavistock Publications.
Erasmus, Charles John
  1950   Patolli, Pachisi and the limitation of possibilities. *Southwestern Journal of Anthropology* 6:369-387.
Evans-Pritchard, E. E.
  1960   *Kinship and marriage among the Nuer.* Oxford: The Clarendon Press.
  1962   *Social anthropology and other essays.* New York: The Free Press.
  1963   *The comparative method in social anthropology.* London: University of London, The Athlone Press.
Feigl, Herbert
  1964   Philosophy of science. In *Philosophy,* eds. R. M. Chisholm et al. Englewood Cliffs, N.J.: Prentice-Hall. (Humanistic Scholarship in America: Princeton Studies etc. by Richard Schlatter.)

Firth, Raymond
   1936   *We, the Tikopia.* London: George Allen and Unwin.
   1951   *Elements of social organization.* London: Watts.
   1959   *Social change in Tikopia: restudy of a Polynesian community after a generation.* New York: The Macmillan Co.
Ford, C. S.
   1945   *A comparative study of human reproduction.* Yale University Publications in Anthropology, No. 32. New Haven, Conn.: Yale University Press.
Ford, C. S. and Frank A. Beach
   1951   *Patterns of sexual behavior.* New York: Harper and Row.
Ford, James A.
   1954   On the concept of types: the type concept revisited. *American Anthropologist* 56:42-53 (especially page 45).
Fortes, Meyer
   1949   Time and social structure: an Ashanti case study. In *Social structure: studies presented to A. R. Radcliffe-Brown,* ed. M. Fortes. Oxford: Clarendon Press.
Fortes, Meyer, ed.
   1949   *Social structure: studies presented to A. R. Radcliffe-Brown.* Oxford: Clarendon Press.
Fortes, Meyer and E. E. Evans-Pritchard, eds.
   1940   *African political systems.* Oxford: Oxford University Press.
Frake, Charles O.
   1964   Notes on queries in anthropology. In Transcultural studies in cognition, eds. A. Kimball Romney and Goodwin D'Andrade. Special Publication, *American Anthropologist* 66(3):132-145.
Freeman, E. A.
   1873   *Comparative politics.* London: Macmillan and Co.
Fried, Morton H.
   1957   The classification of corporate unilineal descent groups. *Journal of the Royal Anthropological Institute* 87:1-29.
Galdwin, Thomas
   1954   Review of J. W. M. Whiting and I. Child's *Child training and personality. American Anthropologist* 56:893-897.
Gluckman, Max
   1950   Kinship and marriage among the Lozi of Northern Rhodesia and the Zulu of Natal. In *African systems of kinship and marriage,* eds. A. R. Radcliffe-Brown and Daryll Forde. Oxford: Oxford University Press for the International African Institute.
   1954   *Rituals of rebellion in south-east Africa.* (The Frazes Lecture, 1952). Manchester: Manchester University Press.
Goethals, George W. and J. W. M. Whiting
   1957   Research methods: the cross-cultural method. *Review of Educational Research* 27:441-448.
Goh, S. T.
   1970   The logic of explanation in anthropology. *Inquiry* 13:339-359.
Goldenweiser, A.
   1918   Form and content in totemism. *American Anthropologist* 20:280-295.
   1931   Totemism: an essay on religion and society. In *The making of man,* ed. V. F. Calverton. New York: Modern Library.
   1933   *History, psychology and culture.* New York: Alfred A. Knopf.
Goldschmidt, Walter
   1966   *Comparative functionalism: essays in anthropological theory.* Berkeley and Los Angeles: University of California Press.

Goldstein, Kurt
    1939   *The organism: a holistic approach to biology derived from pathological data in man.* New York: American Book Company.
Goode, William J. and P. K. Hatt
    1952   *Methods in social research.* New York: McGraw Hill Book Company.
Goody, Jack
    1959   Mother's brother and sister's son in west Africa. *Journal of the Royal Anthropological Institute* 89:61-68.
Gough, E. Kathleen
    1955   Female initiation rites on the Malabar Coast. *Journal of the Royal Anthropological Institute* 85:45-80.
    1965   The Nayars and the definition of marriage. In *Cultural and social anthrolopolgy: selected readings,* ed. Peter B. Hammond. New York: The Macmillan Co.
Graebner, Fritz
    1911   *Methode der ethnologie.* Heidelberg: Winter.
Hammel, E. A.
    1968   Anthropological explanations: style in discourse. *Southwestern Journal of Anthropology* 24:155-169.
Harré, R.
    1965   *An introduction to the logic of the sciences.* London: Macmillan and Co. Ltd.
Heine-Geldern, Robert von
    1954   Die asiatische Herkunft der sudamerikanischen Metalltechnik. *Paideuma* 5:347-423.
Hempel, Carl G.
    1942   The function of general laws in history. *The Journal of Philosophy* 39:35-48 (Reprinted in Patrick Gardiner's, ed. *Theories of history.* Glencoe, Illinois: The Free Press.)
    1952   *Fundamentals of concept formation in empirical science.* Chicago: The University of Chicago Press.
    1962   Deductive-nomological vs. statistical explanation. In *Minnesota studies in the philsopohy of science,* vol. 3, eds. H. Feigl and G. Maxwell. Minneapolis: University of Minnesota Press.
    1964   Explanation in science and in history. In *Frontiers of science and philosophy,* ed. Robert G. Colodny. London: George Allen and Unwin.
    1965   *Aspects of scientific explanation.* New York: The Free Press of Glencoe.
    1969   Scientific explanation. In *Philosophy of science.* Voice of America Forum Lectures. Madras: Higginbothams (P) Limited.
Hempel, Carl G. and Paul Oppenheim
    1948   Studies in the logic of explanation. *Philosophy of Science* 15:135-175. (Reprinted in Hempel 1965.)
Herskovits, M. J.
    1948   *Man and his works.* New York: Alfred A. Knopf.
    1954   Some problems of method in ethnography. In *Method and perspective in anthropology,* ed. R. F. Spencer. Minneapolis: University of Minnesota Press.
Hobhouse, L. T., G. C. Wheeler, and Morris Ginsberg
    1915   *The material culture and social institutions of simpler peoples: an essay in correlation.* London: Chapman and Hall.
Kaplan, Abraham
    1965   *The conduct of inquiry: methodology of behavioral science.* San Francisco: Chandler Publishing Company.

Kaufmann, Felix
  1944   *Methodology of the social sciences.* New York: Oxford University Press.
Klimeck, Stanislaus
  1939   *Culture element distributions: I. The structure of California Indian culture.* University of California Publications in American Archaeology and Ethnology, no. 37. Berkeley: University of California Press.
Kluckhohn, Clyde
  1946   Review of A. L. Kroeber's *Configurations of culture growth. American Journal of Sociology* 51:336-341.
  1954   Culture and behaviour. In *Handbook of social psychology,* vol. 1, ed. Gardner Lindzey. Cambridge, Mass.: Addison-Wesley Publishing Company.
Köbben, A. J.
  1952   The new ways of presenting an old idea: the statistical method in social anthropology. *Journal of the Royal Anthropological Institute* 82:129-146.
Koppers, Wilhelm
  1956   Diffusion: transmission and acceptance. In *Current anthropology,* ed. W. L. Thomas, Jr. Chicago: The University of Chicago Press.
Kotarbinska, Janina
  1962   The controversy: deductivism vs. inductivism. In *Logic, methodology and philosophy of science,* eds. E. Nagel et al. Stanford: Stanford University Press.
Krieger, Alex D.
  1944   The typological concept. *American Antiquity* 9:271-288 (especially page 272).
Kroeber, A. L.
  1931   Historical reconstruction of culture growths and organic evolution. *American Anthropologist* 33:149-151.
  1939   *Cultural and natural areas of native north America.* University of California Publications in American Archaeology and Ethnology, no. 38. Berkeley: University of California Press.
  1944   *Configurations of culture growth.* Berkeley and Los Angeles: University of California Press.
  1948   *Anthropology.* Rev. ed. New York: Harcourt, Brace and Co.
  1952   *The nature of culture.* Chicago: The University of Chicago Press.
  1954   Critical summary and commentary. In *Method and perspective in anthropology,* ed. R. F. Spencer. Minneapolis: University of Minnesota Press.
  1963   *An anthropologist looks at history.* Berkeley and Los Angeles: University of California Press.
Kyburg, Henry E. and Ernest Nagel, eds.
  1963   *Induction: some current issues.* Middletown, Connecticut: Wesleyan University Press.
Leach, E. R.
  1950   Review of G. P. Murdock's *Social structure. Man* 50: no. 169.
  1961a   *Pul Eliya, village in Ceylon: study of land tenure and kinship.* London: Cambridge University Press.
  1961b   *Rethinking anthropology.* London: University of London, The Athlone Press.
  1964   *Political systems of highland Burma.* Boston: Beacon Press.
Lehman, F. K.
  1964   Typology and the classification of socio-cultural systems. In *Process and pattern in culture: essays in honour of Julian H. Steward,* ed. Robert A. Manners. Chicago: Aldine Publishing Company.

Lévi-Strauss, Claude
1963a *Social structure.* New York: Basic Books.
1963b *Totemism.* Boston: Beacon Press.

Lewis, Oscar
1951 *Life in a Mexican village.* Urbana, Illinois: University of Illinois Press.
1953 Controls and experiments in field work. In *Anthropology today,* ed. A. L. Kroeber. Chicago: The University of Chicago Press.
1955 Comparisons in cultural anthropology. In *Year book of anthropology,* 1955, ed. W. L. Thomas, Jr. New York: Wenner-Gren Foundation.

Lowie, Robert H.
1912 On the principle of convergence in ethnology. *Journal of American Folklore* 25:24-42.
1920 *Primitive society.* New York: Boni and Liveright.
1940 *An introduction to cultural anthropology.* New York: Farrar and Rineholt, Inc.

Lundberg, George A.
1953 *Social research: a study in methods of data gathering.* New York: Longmans, Green & Co.

MacIntyre, Alasdair
1967 The idea of a social science. In *The Aristotelian Society supplementary volume XLI (1967).* London: Published for the Aristotelian Society by Harrison & Sons Ltd.

Mair, L. P.
1963 *New nations.* Chicago: The University of Chicago Press.

Malinowski, B.
1944 *A scientiic theory of culture and other essays.* Chapel Hill, N.C.: University of North Carolina Press.
1961 *Argonauts of the western Pacific.* New York: E. P. Dutton & Co., Inc. (Originally published in 1922.)
1963 *The family among the Australian aborigines.* Rev. ed. New York: Schocken Books. (Originally published in 1913.)

Mason, Otis T.
1931 Types of basket weaves. In *Source book in anthropology,* eds. A. L. Kroeber and T. T. Waterman. Rev. ed. New York: Harcourt, Brace and Company.

Mead, Margaret
1968 *Anthropology: a human science.* New Delhi: Affiliated East-West Press Private Limited.

Mill, J. S.
1911 *A system of logic.* London: Longmans, Green and Co.

Montesquieu, Baron de
1748 *De l'esprit des lois.* Geneva. (English translation The Spirit of Laws by T. Nugent, New York, 1949.)

Moore, Frank W., ed.
1961 *Readings in cross-cultural methodology.* New Haven, Conn.: HRAF Press.

Murdock, G. P.
1949 *Social structure.* New York: The Macmillan Company.

Nadel, S. F.
1951 *The foundations of social anthropology.* London: Cohen and West.
1952 Witchcraft in four African societies: an essay in comparison. *American Anthropologist* 54:18-29.

Nader, Laura
1968 Field work. In *Anthropology.* Voice of America Forum Lectures. Madras: Higginbothams (P) Limited.

Nagel, Ernest
 1961 *The structure of science*. New York: Harcourt, Brace and World.
Norbeck, Edward, Donald E. Walker and Mimi Cohen
 1962 The interpretation of data: puberty rites. *American Anthropologist* 64:463-485.
Northrop, F. S. C.
 1964 Toward a deductively-formulated and operationally verifiable comparative cultural anthropology. In *Cross-cultural understanding: epistemology in anthropology,* eds. F. S. C. Northrop and H. H. Livingston. New York: Harper and Row.
Pelto, Pertti J.
 1970 *Anthropological research: the structure of inquiry*. New York: Harper and Row.
Peter, Prince of Greece and Denmark
 1963 *A study of polyandry*. The Hague: Mouton and Co.
Popper, Karl
 1959 *The logic of scientific discovery*. New York: Basic Books.
Powdermaker, H.
 1968 Field work. In *International encyclopedia of the social sciences,* ed. David L. Sills, vol. 5: 418-424. New York: The Macmillan Company and the Free Press.
Radcliffe-Brown, A. R.
 1924 The mother's brother in South Africa. *South African Journal of Science* XXI: 542-55. (Reprinted in *Structure and function in primitive society.* 1952. Glencoe, Illinois: The Free Press.)
 1929 The sociological theory of totemism. Proceedings of the Fourth Pacific Science Congress, Java. (Reprinted in *Structure and function in primitive society.* 1952. Glencoe, Illinois: The Free Press.)
 1930-31 Social organization of Australian tribes. *Oceania* I:34-63; 206-246; 322-341 and 426-456.
 1951 On the comparative method in social anthropology. *Journal of the Royal Anthropological Institute* 81:15-22. (Reprinted in *Method in social anthropology.* 1958. Chicago: The University of Chicago Press.)
 1952 *Structure and function in primitive society*. London: Cohen and West.
 1958 *Method in social anthropology,* ed. R. A. Manners. Chicago: The University of Chicago Press.
Radcliffe-Brown, A. R. and Daryll Forde, eds.
 1950 *African systems of kinship and marriage*. London: Oxford University Press for International African Institute.
Redfield, Robert
 1941 *The folk-culture of Yucatan*. Chicago: The University of Chicago Press.
 1950 *A village that chose progress: Chan Kom revisited*. Chicago: The University of Chicago Press.
 1954 *The primitive world and its transformations*. Ithaca: Cornell University Press.
 1957 The cultural role of cities. *Economic Development and Cultural Change* 3:53-73.
 1962 *Human nature and the study of society*. Papers of Robert Redfield, vol. I, ed. Margaret Park Redfield. Chicago: The University of Chicago Press.
Rescher, Nicholas
 1963 Fundamental problems in the theory of scientific explanation. In *Philosophy of science: The Dalaware seminar,* vol. 2 (1962-1963), ed. Bernard Baumrin. New York: Interscience Publishers.

Richards, A. I.
    1950   Some types of family structure amongst the central Bantu. In *African systems of kinship and marriage,* eds. A. R. Radcliffe-Brown and Daryll Forde. London: Oxford University Press.

Ritchie, A. D.
    1960   *Studies in the history and methods of the sciences.* Edinburgh: The University Press.

Rouse, Irving
    1939   *Prehistory in Haiti, a study in method.* Yale University Publications in Anthropology, no. 21. New Haven, Conn.: Yale University Press.

Śaraṇa, Gopāla
    1965   On comparative methods in social-cultural anthropology and in linguistics. *Anthropological Quarterly* 38:20-40.
    1968   Some observations on the definition of marriage. *Ethnos* (1968):159-167.
    In   The methodology of a structuralist, mimeographed. (To be published
    press   in *Anthropology of Claude Lévi-Strauss,* eds. H. G. Nutini and I. R. Buchler. New York: Appleton-Century Crofts.)

Schapera, Isaac
    1953   Some comments on comparative method in social anthropology. *American Anthropologist* 55:353-362.

Scheffler, Israel
    1957   Explanation, prediction and abstraction. *British Journal for the Philosophy of Science* 7:293-309.
    1963   *The anatomy of inquiry: philosophical studies in the theory of science.* New York: Alfred A. Knopf.

Schmidt, Wilhelm
    1939   *The cultural historical method of ethnology: the scientific approach to the racial question.* S. A. Sieber, trans. New York: Fortuney's.

Scriven, Michael
    1958   Definitions, explanations and theories. In *Minnesota studies in philosophy of science,* vol. 2, eds. H. Feigl, M. Scriven and G. Maxwell. Minneapolis: University of Minnesota Press.
    1959   Truism as the grounds of historical explanations. In *Theories of history,* ed. Patrick Gardiner. Glencoe, Illinois: The Free Press.
    1962   Explanations, predictions and laws. In *Minnesota studies in the philosophy of science,* vol. 3, eds. H. Feigl and G. Maxwell. Minneapolis: University of Minnesota Press.

Selltiz, Claire et al.
    1962   *Research methods in social relations.* New York: Holt, Rinehart and Winston.

Smith, M. G.
    1962   *West Indian family structure.* Seattle, Washington: University of Washington Press.

Spaulding, Albert C.
    1953   Statistical techniques for the discovery of artifact types. *American Antiquity* 18:305-313 (especially page 305).
    1968   Explanation in archaeology. In *New perspectives in archaeology,* eds. Sally R. Binford and L. R. Binford. Chicago: Aldine Publishing Company.

Spier, Leslie
    1921   The sun dance of the Plains Indians. American Museum of Natural History, Anthropological Papers, 16. New York.

Steward, Julian H.
    1954   Type of types. *American Anthropologist* 56:54-57.

1955   *The theory of culture change.* Urbana, Illinois: University of Illinois Press.

Tax, Sol et al., eds.
1953   *An appraisal of anthropology today.* Chicago: The University of Chicago Press.

Thorndike, Lynn
1969   Renaissance. *Encyclopaedia Britannica* 19:122-129. Chicago: Encyclopaedia Britannica Inc.

Tylor, E. B.
1871   *Primitive culture: researches into the development of mythology, philosophy, religion, language, art and custom.* 2 vol. London: John Murray.
1878   On the game of Patolli in ancient Mexico, and its probable Asiatic origin. *Journal of the Royal Anthropological Institute.*
1895   *Anthropology: an introduction to the study of man and civilization.* London: Macmillan.
1896   On American lot-games as evidence of Asiatic intercourse before the time of Columbus. *Internationales Archiv fur Ethnographie* 9: suppl.: *Ethnographische Britrage.*

Voltaire
1819   *Essai sur les moeurs et l'esprit des nations.* Paris: A. A. Renouard.

Von Wright, Georg Henrik
1957   *The logical problem of induction.* 2nd rev. ed. New York: The Macmillan Company.

Weber, Max
1947   *The theory of social and economic organization.* A. M. Henderson and Talcott Parsons, trans. New York: Oxford University Press.
1949   *On the methodology of social sciences.* E. A. Shils and H. D. Finch, trans. New York: The Free Press of Glencoe.

Whewell, William
1897   *History of the inductive sciences from the earliest to the present time.* 3rd ed. New York: D. Appleton and Company.

White, Leslie A.
1946   Kroeber's configurations of culture growth. *American Anthropologist* 48:78-93.

Whiting, Beatrice, ed.
1963   *Six cultures: studies of child rearing.* New York: Wiley.

Whiting, J. W. M.
1954   The cross-cultural method. In *Handbook of social psychology,* vol. 1, ed. Gardner Lindzey. Cambridge, Mass.: Addison-Wesley Publishing Company.
1961   Socialization process and personality. In *Psychological anthropology,* ed. Francis L. K. Hsu. Homewood, Illinois: The Dorsey Press, Inc.

Whiting, J. W. M. and I. L. Child
1953   *Child training and personality: a cross-cultural study.* New Haven, Conn.: Yale University Press.

Wilson, Godfrey and Monica
1945   *The analysis of social change, based on observations in central Africa.* Cambridge, England: The University Press.

Winch, Peter
1958   *The idea of a social science: and its relation to philosophy.* London: Routledge & Kegan Paul.

Wissler, Clark
1923   The universal pattern. In *Man and culture.* New York: Thomas Y. Crowell.

1926   *The relation of nature to man in aboriginal America.* New York: Oxford University Press.

Wolf, A.
1962   *Textbook of logic.* New York: Collier Books.

Woodhouse, A. S. P.
1969   Humanities. *Encyclopaedia Britannica* 2: 826-827. Chicago: Encyclopaedia Britannica Inc.